ECONOMISTS' PAPERS 1750–1950

THE COMMITTEE OF THE
GUIDE TO ARCHIVE SOURCES IN THE HISTORY
OF ECONOMIC THOUGHT

R. D. COLLISON BLACK
Professor of Economics
The Queen's University of Belfast

A. W. COATS
Professor of Economic and Social History
University of Nottingham

B. A. CORRY
Professor of Economics
Queen Mary College, London

R. H. ELLIS
formerly Secretary of the
Royal Commission on Historical Manuscripts

LORD ROBBINS
formerly Professor of Economics
University of London

D. N. WINCH
Professor of Economics
University of Sussex

ECONOMISTS' PAPERS 1750—1950

A Guide to Archive and other Manuscript Sources for the History of British and Irish Economic Thought

Compiled for the Committee of the
Guide to Archive Sources in the History of
Economic Thought by

R. P. STURGES

DUKE UNIVERSITY PRESS
Durham, N.C.
1975

First published 1975 by
The Macmillan Press Ltd

Library of Congress Catalogue Card Number 75–2611

ISBN 8223–0337–X

Printed in Great Britain

CONTENTS

INTRODUCTION

There has recently been a significant expansion of research and publication in the history of economic thought. The number of reprints of economic classics has grown apace, major biographical studies and scholarly editions have appeared or are in process, and the flow of historical or interpretative monographs and scholarly articles has steadily increased. Moreover, it is evident that this resurgence of interest and activity will continue in the foreseeable future. Antiquarian motives have, inevitably, played a part in this movement; but questions of considerable importance and current concern to a number of disciplines are also involved, which go beyond the history of economic theory, techniques and their applications to include the relations between economic ideas and policy, and the history, sociology and general cultural significance of economics and related social sciences as manifestations of the development of intellectual professions in modern society.

Recent improvements in the quality of the research undertaken in the history of economics, requiring in those who undertake it a full command of the techniques of the historian as well as of economic analysis, have led to an increased interest in the use of manuscript material. This has brought to light serious deficiencies in the preservation, cataloguing and publicising of such materials, and emphasised the need for a systematic guide to sources of this kind in Britain. Although several guides to printed materials exist,[1] there is no single specialist index to the papers of economists. In an effort to remedy these deficiencies a committee of members of an informal international History of Economic Thought group based in Britain decided to launch a systematic enquiry into the location and condition of the surviving papers of British economists who lived in the period 1700–

[1] For example, the *Catalogue of the Kress Library*, the *London Bibliography of the Social Sciences*, the *Catalogue of the Goldsmiths' Library of Economic Literature*, vol. I (Cambridge, 1970), and Henry Higgs' *Bibliography of Economics, 1751–1775* (Cambridge, 1935).

1950. The present *Guide to Archive Sources* represents the fruits of this endeavour.

The committee responsible for the Guide comprised Professor R. D. Collison Black, Queen's University, Belfast (Chairman); and Professors A. W. Coats, University of Nottingham; Bernard Corry, Queen Mary College, London; and Donald N. Winch, University of Sussex. Expert assistance was provided by Mr Roger H. Ellis, then Secretary of the Historical Manuscripts Commission, while Lord Robbins acted as a general adviser. The project was made possible by generous grants from the Social Science Research Council and the Royal Economic Society. With the aid of these funds a full-time Research Assistant, Mr Paul Sturges, was employed for three years from 1 August 1970, in the work of locating and recording the details of the surviving manuscript sources. The committee would like to take this opportunity of thanking the Royal Economic Society and the Social Science Research Council for their support of the project, as well as the many librarians, archivists and other colleagues who freely gave expert assistance during the course of the work, and the Director and staff of the University of London's Institute of Historical Research who provided accommodation and other facilities for Mr Sturges during his tenure of the Research Assistantship. The committee also wish to record their appreciation of Mr Sturges' unfailing enthusiasm and dedication to the project.

The first task of the committee was to agree on a list of economists in the period since 1700 whose influence and general reputation would justify the location and recording of any of their surviving papers. Before Mr Sturges began his work the committee had already compiled a list of over four hundred British economic writers who might fall into this category. This compilation inevitably presented certain problems, given the difficulty of defining the term 'economist', particularly in more distant times.

The next, more important, step was to decide what type of survey to carry out. Two types can be distinguished: a broad one dealing mainly with personal papers of a great number of people, or a more intensive one which attempts to list the personal papers and correspondence of a more select group. The former is exemplified by Roy McCleod's *Archives of British Men of Science* (Mansell, 1972, microfiche), and the latter by John Brooke, *The Prime Ministers' Papers, 1801–1902* (H.M.S.O.,

1968). After discussion and consultation, the latter was adopted as a model. A major consideration in this choice was the significance of correspondence in the development, modification and dissemination of economic ideas. The latter type of survey provides more detailed information on correspondence.

A brief account of the procedures adopted in preparing this Guide may be helpful both to its users and to those embarking upon similar projects in the future. The initial list of economists provided a basis for the collection of biographical data and a search of the published literature for clues to the whereabouts of known collections. A check of the indexes and lists at the National Register of Archives proved especially helpful at this stage, and was followed by the despatch of letters to institutions known to hold relevant papers, and specific enquiries to other likely institutions. Wherever the response was positive, visits were undertaken, beginning with the major London repositories – such as the British Museum, London School of Economics, University College, etc. – and subsequently extending to other parts of the British Isles. Where possible, information was taken from the repositories' own lists and indexes and, where necessary, from the actual collections. In cases where the collections were large and ill-organised, or where lists and indexes were poor, full information as to the contents was sometimes unobtainable at the time. After about sixteen months the majority of visits to repositories had been completed, and serious efforts were then made to trace papers as yet unknown or unused by scholars, especially those in private hands. Investigations of a largely genealogical character, centring on wills at the General Register Office at Somerset House, and utilising a wide range of directories and biographical dictionaries, had already been initiated in between visits to repositories. And as these visits declined in frequency the genealogical investigations were increased. Whenever the descendants of economists were traced they were approached by letter and, if appropriate, a visit was arranged. The results of these enquiries were often negative, either because nothing had survived, or because the families had died out or disappeared leaving no clues to the fate of the economist's papers. Nevertheless, the Guide gives some indications of these negative cases and will therefore save the time and energy of future researchers. The project has confirmed the general impression, gained from the results of other surveys and conversations with archivists, that investigations of this kind, though very demanding in time and effort, succeed in disclosing only a very small proportion of entirely new material. They do, however, perform a valuable function by drawing together in one place widely scattered and sometimes forgotten information about papers in private hands. The hope may be expressed that distinguished living persons will consider bequeathing their papers to some of the major libraries where they can be properly preserved and made available to posterity.

Nature of the Guide and directions for its use

This Guide contains a finding list of personal papers and correspondence of the most distinguished British economists, as well as a considerable number of lesser contributors to the subject in one or other of its forms. The lists printed here comprise all those cases where a significant body of material is known to exist, whatever its content. Indeed, in a few cases, such as Isaac Butt and Fleeming Jenkin, little or nothing of what is listed is directly economic in content. The individuals listed include personalities from the universities, banking, business, politics, the Civil Service, journalism and other fields. The Guide will therefore be useful not only to specialist historians of economics, but also to all concerned with the role of economic ideas in political debate, public and private decision-making, and in the formation of public opinion. Some of the supplementary information compiled but not published herein will be available to enquirers at the National Register of Archives, Quality House, Quality Court, Chancery Lane, London WC2A 1HP.

Wherever possible, three main types of information have been recorded:

1. A brief description of the main group or groups of personal papers which the economist accumulated during his lifetime. It indicates the nature of the material (e.g. whether in-letters, drafts, or copies of out-letters, manuscripts of published or unpublished works, diaries, memoranda, etc.); period of origin; quantity; and, if relevant, the state of preservation or organisation. Reference is also made to many of the artificial collections of papers relating to prominent figures assembled or acquired by libraries, usually after the subject's death. The geographical location of the material listed is largely confined to Great

Britain and Ireland, with some additions from the more obvious sources on the continents of Europe and North America. The locations of collections are indicated (*a*) by name of repository in abbreviated form; (*b*) N.R.A. numbers, where appropriate (see list of N.R.A. numbers on p. xxi); (*c*) footnote-type numbers (see list of these on p. xxii).

2. A list of persons to whom the economist wrote, information as to the whereabouts of his out-letters and, where possible, an indication of the numbers and period of the surviving correspondence. For eight economists (David Hume, Jevons, J. M. Keynes, Smith, Bentham, Burke, Ricardo and J. S. Mill) this section is omitted as extensive editions of their correspondence are now complete or in progress, and provide much fuller lists than could be offered here.
3. A brief note of the principal published works largely or wholly consisting of material from the economist's papers, including substantial biographies and other printed works using or containing references to his papers. References to articles in five major biographical dictionaries and encyclopaedias are given in abbreviated form, and there is some information as to the whereabouts of the subject's portrait.

In the case of the first and last of these categories, no comments are required. In the case of category 2, however, it should be noted that limitations of time made it impossible to trace all the economist's letters which might exist in the possession of the descendants of his known or presumed correspondents. Consequently, many more groups of letters are listed for the major nineteenth-century figures, some of whom were more famous outside the field of economics, than for more recent or less well-known individuals. Since many lists and indexes omit this information, it has not always been possible to indicate the quantity and the period of groups of letters. However, some indication of the numbers has been provided, and the terms 'a few', 'several' and 'many' may be taken as roughly equivalent to 'two or three', 'about a dozen' and 'more than a dozen' respectively. The term 'items' includes letters, enclosures, drafts of replies, etc.

The most important class of records omitted is that contained in the Public Records Office. Collections of politicians' papers given to or deposited with the P.R.O. are referred to in so far as the P.R.O.'s indexes permit. But it has not been possible to undertake a systematic search through the papers of a relevant ministry or department to trace the letters and memoranda of an economist who was employed there. Research workers are, however, advised to examine the papers of government departments where appropriate, as these often constitute rich sources of material. The Bank of England is another important source which has not been investigated for the purposes of this Guide, but the Court has authorised the statement included in the footnote below.[2]

Notes for those using the Guide

1. The Guide is designed to assist the research worker at the beginning of his enquiries by enabling him to find the items listed and obtain some idea of their size and scope. It does no more to reveal the contents of any collection. The reader is advised that lists of the kind provided herein can never be exhaustive, and those who wish to obtain as complete a coverage of the manuscript material as possible will look beyond these pages.
2. The Guide does not distinguish between papers owned by a library or repository and those merely loaned or depo-

[2] 'The records of the Bank were extensively used by Sir John Clapham when writing his history, *The Bank of England*, 2 vols (Cambridge University Press, 1944) and its footnotes, appendices and index furnish a readily accessible guide. The main series consists of:

(i) Minute Books of the General Court of Proprietors
(ii) Minute Books of the Court of Directors
(iii) Minute Books of the Committee of Treasury
(iv) Letter Books
(v) General Ledgers
(vi) Drawing Office Ledgers

all of which, with the exception of (iii) and (iv), date from 1694, the year of the Bank's foundation.

The records are a working archive for the daily business of the Bank itself, but access to them may be given to historians and research workers provided that they either are known to the Bank or are suitably sponsored. In the normal course, access to records which are less than 100 years old is not allowed, although consideration would always be given to a specific enquiry falling within that period.

Applications should be addressed to the Secretary.'

sited there by the owners or their trustees. In the latter case, permission to publish material from the papers will be required from both the library and the owner; and in certain cases the owner's permission will be required before the papers can be viewed. It is therefore advisable to enquire about the accessibility of papers before visiting a collection.

3. Some collections are privately owned and retained in the owner's private residence or business premises. A reference to a collection in the Guide does not necessarily mean that the owner is prepared to grant access to each and every enquirer. Wherever possible, an indication of the conditions under which the owners are prepared to grant access has been given below.
4. Finally, research workers are reminded of the need to familiarise themselves with the law of copyright. Descendants of an individual listed herein may retain copyright in his out-letters even when the item concerned forms part of the recipient's archive and is legally the possession of the present owners of the archive.

LIST OF ECONOMISTS

(Asterisks indicate those for whom a list is not included in this volume.)

Anderson, James
Ashley, Sir W. J.
*Ashton, T. S.
*Attwood, Matthias
Attwood, Thomas

Babbage, Charles
Bagehot, Walter
*Bailey, Samuel
Baring, Alexander, Lord Ashburton
Baring, Sir Francis
Barton, John
Bastable, C. F.
Bentham, Jeremy
Bonar, James
Bowley, Sir A. L.
*Bray, Charles
Bray, John Francis
Burke, Edmund
Butt, Isaac

Cairnes, J. E.
Cannan, Edwin
*Cantillon, Richard
Chalmers, Thomas
Chapman, Sir S. J.
Clapham, Sir J. H.
Cobbett, William
Cobden, Richard
*Collet, Clara
*Craig, John
*Cunningham, William

Eden, Sir F. M.
Edgeworth, F. Y.
Ellis, William

Fawcett, Henry
Ferguson, Adam
*Forster, Nathaniel
Foxwell, H. S.
*Fullarton, John

Giffen, Sir Robert
Goschen, George Joachim, Lord Goschen
Graham, Sir J. R. G.
*Gray, Sir Alexander
*Gray, John
*Gregory, T. E. G.

*Hall, Charles
Hancock, William Neilson
Henderson, Sir Hubert
Higgs, Henry
Hirst, F. W.
Hobson, John Atkinson
Hodgskin, Thomas
Horner, Francis
Hume, David

Hume, James Deacon
Hume, Joseph
Huskisson, William
*Hutcheson, Francis

Ingram, John Kells

*Jacob, William
Jenkin, H. C. Fleeming
Jevons, W. S.
Jones, Richard
Joplin, Thomas

Keynes, John Maynard, Lord Keynes
Keynes, John Neville
*King, W. T. C.

*Lalor, John
*Lavington, Frederick
*Law, John
Leslie, T. E. Cliffe
Levi, Leone
*Lloyd, W. F.
*Longe, F. D.
*Longfield, Mountifort
Lowe, Robert, Lord Sherbrooke
Loyd, S. J., Lord Overstone

McCulloch, J. R.
*Macdonell, Sir John
*MacGregor, D. H.
Macleod, H. D.
Maitland, James, Lord Lauderdale
Mallet, Sir Louis
Malthus, T. R.
*Marcet, Jane
Marshall, Alfred
Martineau, Harriet

Merivale, Herman
Mill, James
Mill, John Stuart
Millar, John
*Munro, J. E. C.

Newmarch, William
Nicholson, J. Shield

Owen, Robert

Palgrave, Sir R. H. I.
*Palmer, John Horsley
Parnell, Henry Brooke, Lord Congleton
Pennington, James
Pigou, A. C.
Place, Francis
Porter, G. R.
Price, Bonamy
Price, Richard

*Rae, John
*Read, Samuel
Ricardo, David
*Robertson, D. H.
Rogers, J. E. Thorold
Rose, George

Scott, W. R.
Scrope, G. P.
Senior, Nassau W.
*Shaw, W. A.
Sidgwick, Henry
Sinclair, Sir John
*Smart, William
Smith, Adam
*Spence, William
Spencer, Herbert
Spring-Rice, T., Lord Monteagle

Steuart-Denham, Sir James
Stewart, Dugald

Tawney, R. H.
Thompson, T. Perronet
*Thompson, William
Thompson, C. E. P., Lord Sydenham
Thornton, Henry
Tooke, Thomas
Torrens, Robert
*Townsend, Joseph
*Toynbee, Arnold

*Unwin, George

Wakefield, Edward
Wakefield, Edward Gibbon
*Wallace, Robert
Webb, S. J.
*West, Sir Edward
Whately, Richard
*Whale, P. B.
*Wheatley, John
Whewell, William
Wicksteed, P. H.
Wilmot-Horton, Sir R. J.
Wilson, James
*Withers, Hartley

Young, Arthur

LIST OF ABBREVIATIONS

B.M.	British Museum
B.M.(P)	British Museum, Department of Prints and Drawings
Boase	F. Boase, *Modern English Biography*, 6 vols. re-issue (London, 1965)
Bodleian	Bodleian Library, Oxford
DNB	*Dictionary of National Biography*, ed. Leslie Stephen and Sidney Lee, 22 vols., re-issue (1908–1909) and Supplements
Durham D.P.	Durham University, Department of Palaeography
ESS	*Encyclopaedia of the Social Sciences*, ed. Edwin R. A. Seligman and Alvin Johnson, 15 vols. (New York, 1930)
IESS	*International Encyclopaedia of the Social Sciences*, ed. David L. Sills, 17 vols. (New York, 1968)
L.S.E.	British Library of Political and Economic Science, London School of Economics
Manchester J.R.U.L.	Manchester, John Rylands University Library
N.L.I.	National Library of Ireland
N.L.S.	National Library of Scotland
N.L.W.	National Library of Wales
N.P.G.	National Portrait Gallery
N.P.G.(A)	National Portrait Gallery (Archives)
N.R.A.	National Register of Archives
Palgrave	R. H. I. Palgrave, *Dictionary of Political Economy* (London, 1894)
P.R.O.	Public Record Office
P.R.O.N.I.	Public Record Office of Northern Ireland

R.O.	Record Office
S.N.G.	Scottish National Gallery
S.N.P.G.	Scottish National Portrait Gallery
U.C.L.	University College London
U.L.	University Library

DETAILS OF PRIVATE COLLECTIONS CITED IN TEXT BY N.R.A. NUMBER

The N.R.A. Reports on these collections provide further details, especially as to access. They can be consulted at the N.R.A.'s Search Room, Quality House, Quality Court, Chancery Lane, London WC2A 1HP. There are also N.R.A. Reports on many of the other collections cited in the text which are held by public institutions.

0001 MSS. of the Earl of Buckinghamshire, Hampden House, Great Hampden, Buckinghamshire.

0842 Disraeli papers. Application should be made by letter to The National Trust, Hughenden Manor, near High Wycombe, Buckinghamshire.

1019 Ruggles-Brise papers. Application should be made initially to the County Archivist of Essex.

1561 Harrowby papers. Earl of Harrowby, Sandon Hall, Stafford. The N.R.A. Report should be consulted for special conditions.

2634 Graham papers. Sir Fergus Graham, Bt, Netherby, Longtown, Cumberland.

8128 Hickleton papers. Enquiries to Lord Halifax's Archivist Major T. L. Ingram, 10 Wellesley Avenue, London W6 0UP.

8681 Lowe papers. Mrs R. T. Sneyd, The Malt House, Hinton Charterhouse, near Bath.

9954 Adam papers. Enquiries to The Secretary, National Register of Archives (Scotland).

10169 Home MSS. Enquiries to The Secretary, National Register of Archives (Scotland).

10172 Hope of Luffness papers. Enquiries to The Secretary, National Register of Archives (Scotland).

10410 Spencer papers. The Earl Spencer, Althorp, Northamptonshire.

10552 Sinclair of Ulbster papers. Enquiries to The Secretary, National Register of Archives (Scotland).

10832 Gourock Ropeworks Co. papers. Enquiries to The Secretary, National Register of Archives (Scotland).

11184 Lambton papers. The Estate Agent, Lambton Estate Office, Lambton Park, Chester-le-Street, Co. Durham.

11630 Mackenzie papers. Enquiries to The Secretary, National Register of Archives (Scotland).

12396 Thorold Rogers papers. Dr M. A. T. Rogers, Secretary, Royal Institution of Great Britain, 21 Albemarle Street, London W1X 4BS.

12609 Crawford papers. Enquiries to The Secretary, National Register of Archives (Scotland).

12889 Broadlands papers. Enquiries to The Secretary, National Register of Archives.

14863 Papers of the Labour Party. The Librarian, Transport House, Smith Square, London SW1

15719 Petworth House Archives. Applications, at least one week in advance, to West Sussex R.O.

16603 Jenkin papers. Patrick Jenkin, M.P., 9 Hurst Avenue, Highgate, London N6

DETAILS OF PRIVATE COLLECTIONS CITED IN TEXT BY NUMBER

Attwood papers[1] Torlesse papers[1] Wakefield papers[1]	Mrs Priscilla Williams 100 Coleherne Court Old Brompton Road London SW5
Bagehot papers[2]	Norman St John-Stevas, M.P. House of Commons London SW1

Bickerdike papers[3]	Dr G. A. Dick Darwin College Cambridge
Clapham papers[4]	Sir Michael Clapham 26 Hill Street London W1
Saltmarsh papers[5]	Personal files of Mr John Saltmarsh King's College Cambridge
Mallet papers[6]	P. L. V. Mallet, Esq. c/o Foreign and Commonwealth Office Mr Mallet is prepared to consider granting access to suitably qualified scholars.
Edgeworth papers[7]	Dr D. E. Butler Nuffield College Oxford OX1 1NF
Collet papers[8]	W. R. Collet, Esq. 13 Roy Road Northwood Middlesex
Palgrave papers[9]	G. P. Barker, Esq. 15 Neville Court Abbey Road London NW8 9DD
William Ritchie's MSS.[10]	Scotsman Publications Ltd 20 North Bridge Edinburgh 1
Macleod papers[11]	Misses E. A. and M.L. Macleod Ardvreck 34 Newton Road Cambridge CB2 2AL
Congleton papers[12]	Lord Congleton Ebbesbourne Wake near Salisbury Wiltshire
Clark papers[13]	Personal files of Dr Colin Clark Mannix College

	Monash University Clayton 3168 Victoria, Australia (Photocopies in the Marshall Library, Cambridge)
Baring Bros. Archives[14]	The Archivist Baring Bros. & Co. Ltd 8 Bishopsgate London EC2
Archives of the Equitable Life Assurance Society[15]	Equitable Life Assurance Society 4 Coleman Street London EC2
Lauderdale MSS.[16]	Capt. the Hon. G. F. I. Maitland Carew Thirlestane Castle Lauder Berwickshire Consult N.R.A. (Scotland) for access.
Archives of John Murray Ltd[17]	John Murray Ltd 50 Albermarle Street London W1X 4BD
Kinnordy MSS.[18]	Lord Lyell Petersham Mews London SW7
Royal Statistical Society[19]	It is necessary to apply in advance by letter to the Secretary for permission to use the Library.

ECONOMISTS' PAPERS 1750–1950

JAMES ANDERSON, 1739–1808

His papers do not seem to have survived; there is a tradition suggesting that his widow burnt them to singe her chickens.

Manuscripts of two papers submitted to the Royal Society for publication in 1780 and 1781.
Royal Society Library, London.

A few letters to and from various correspondents.
Edinburgh U.L.

Correspondents

SIR JOSEPH BANKS, one letter, 1794.
B.M. Add. MS. 33979.

JEREMY BENTHAM, one letter, 1781.
Shelburne papers, W. L. Clements Library, University of Michigan, Ann Arbor.

GEORGE CUMBERLAND, eight letters, 1800–1805.
B.M. Add. MSS. 36498–36500.

GEORGE DEMPSTER, four letters, 1784–1785.
N.L.S., MS. 6602.

DAVID ERSKINE, 11th Earl of Buchan, a few letters, 1767–1796.
Laing MSS., Edinburgh U.L.

JOHN JAY, five items, 1794–1795.
Jay papers, Columbia U.L., New York.

GRIM JONSSON THORKELIN, four letters, 1788-1792.
Edinburgh U.L.

Printed Material

CHARLES F. MULLETT, 'A Village Aristotle and the Harmony of Interests: James Anderson (1739–1808) of Monks Hill', *Journal of British Studies*, VIII 1 (1968) 94.

Palgrave I 39; *DNB* I 381; *ESS* II 55.

Portrait: B.M. (P); N.P.G. (A).

SIR WILLIAM JAMES ASHLEY, 1860–1927

Ashley's papers, as used in Anne Ashley's biography (see below), do not seem to have survived.

Letters and other papers connected with his work for various official bodies during and after the 1914–1918 war.
B.M. Add. MSS. 42242–42256.

Letter books, containing *c.* 500 out-letters, 1918–1921, written in his capacity as Vice-Principal of Birmingham University.
Birmingham University Archives.

Correspondents

HENRY CARTER ADAMS, five letters, 1895–1900.
Adams papers, Michigan Historical Collections, University of Michigan, Ann Arbor.

AMERICAN ECONOMIC ASSOCIATION, letters to and from, 1888–1910.
A.E.A. papers, Northwestern University, Evanston, Illinois.

WILLIAM HENRY BEVERIDGE, Baron Beveridge, one or two letters, 1925.
Beveridge papers, L.S.E.

EDWIN CANNAN, seven letters, 1896–1925.
Cannan collection, L.S.E.

RICHARD THEODORE ELY, a few letters, 1888–1900.
Ely papers, University of Wisconsin, Madison.

JOHN LAWRENCE LE BRETON HAMMOND, five letters, 1913–1926.
Bodleian, MS. Hammond.

JOHN MAYNARD KEYNES, Baron Keynes, nine letters, 1912–1921.
Keynes papers, Marshall Library, Cambridge.

EDWIN ROBERT ANDERSON SELIGMAN, 60 letters, 1887–1909.
Seligman collection, Columbia U.L., New York.

GOLDWIN SMITH, five letters, 1890–1895.
Goldwin Smith papers, Cornell U.L., Ithaca, New York.

GRAHAM WALLAS, four letters, 1897–1903.
Wallas papers, L.S.E.

Printed Material

ANNE ASHLEY, *William James Ashley: A Life* (London, 1932).

H. W. MCCREADY, 'Sir William Ashley: Some Unpublished Letters', *Journal of Economic History*, xv (1955) 34–43.

DNB 1922–1930, 27; *ESS* II 268; *IESS* I 411.

Portrait: see biography by Anne Ashley (above).

THOMAS ATTWOOD, 1783–1856

Attwood's correspondence with his wife, 1803–1839, in four boxes, a volume of copies of Attwood's correspondence, 1803–1848 (mainly with his wife, but some with others), scrapbooks and copies of Attwood's published works.
Attwood papers.[1]

A group of six letters to Attwood, and two drafts of letters by him, 1812–1843.
Attwood–Hadley papers, London U.L., MS. 642 and A.L. 260.

Correspondents

HENRY PETER BROUGHAM, 1st Baron Brougham and Vaux, six letters, 1812–1842.
Brougham papers, U.C.L.

EDWARD DAVIES DAVENPORT, 17 letters, 1822–1830.
Bromley-Davenport Muniments, Manchester J.R.U.L.

JOHN CAM HOBHOUSE, Baron Broughton, three letters, 1830.
B.M. Add. MS. 36466.

ROBERT BANKS JENKINSON, 2nd Earl of Liverpool, five letters, 1812–1819.
B.M. Add. MSS. 38277–38410.

SIR ROBERT PEEL, 10 items, 1825–1844.
B.M. Add. MSS. 40384–40551.

SIR GEORGE SINCLAIR, *c.* 12 letters, 1836–1848.
Sinclair of Ulbster papers, N.R.A. 10552.

Printed Material

C. M. WAKEFIELD, *Life of Thomas Attwood* (London, 1885).

FRANK WHITSON FETTER, *Selected Economic Writings of Thomas Attwood* (London, 1964).

Palgrave I 67; *DNB* XXII 86; Boase I 105; *ESS* II 307.

Portrait: B.M. (P); N.P.G. (A).

CHARLES BABBAGE, 1792–1871

Correspondence, mainly on scientific matters, but including some on economics and politics, from 1806–1871, with drafts of many of his own letters and some scientific papers.
B.M. Add. MSS. 37182–37205.

Manuscripts of five scientific papers, 1815–1826, and letters and papers of three committees, 1823, 1829 and 1831, on the Calculating Engine.
Royal Society Library, London.

Small groups of scientific papers and correspondence.
The Libraries of the Science Museum, London; the Royal Astronomical Society, London; Oxford University Museum of the History of Science; and the Cambridge Philosophical Society.

Correspondents

JAMES DAVID FORBES, eight letters and six replies, 1831–1855.
Forbes correspondence, St Andrews U.L.

GEORGE HAMILTON GORDON, 4th Earl of Aberdeen, three items of correspondence, 1844.
B.M. Add. MS. 43243.

SIR JOHN FREDERICK WILLIAM HERSCHEL, 400 items of correspondence, 1812–1866.
Herschel papers, Royal Society Library, London.

SIR JOHN WILLIAM LUBBOCK, 25 letters, 1829–1860.
Lubbock papers, Royal Society Library, London.

SIR CHARLES LYELL, six letters, 1832.
American Philosophical Association Library, Philadelphia.

SIR ROBERT PEEL, five items of correspondence, 1822–1842.
B.M. Add. MSS. 40350–40516.

ADOLPHE QUÉTELET, 15 letters, 1826–1862.
Quételet papers, Bibliothèque Royale de Belgique, Brussels.

WILLIAM SOMERVILLE, 34 letters, 1828–1837.
Somerville papers, Bodleian.

CHARLES SUMNER, two letters, 1838.
Houghton Library, Harvard University.

WILLIAM WHEWELL, four letters, 1820–1848.
Whewell papers, Trinity College, Cambridge.

Printed Material

MABOTH MOSELEY, *Irascible Genius: A Life of Charles Babbage* (London, 1964).

Palgrave I 75; *DNB* I 776; Boase I 116; *ESS* II 374; *IESS* I 491.

Portraits: B.M. (P); N.P.G.; and Moseley (see above).

WALTER BAGEHOT, 1826–1877

A small collection of letters, 1838–1875, mainly to his father and mother before 1850, but with some to R. H. Hutton.
Bagehot papers.[2]

Ten notebooks from lectures at University College, London, 1842–1844.
U.C.L.

Eight letters to Bagehot, and Mrs Bagehot, from W. E. Gladstone, 1861–1881.
Giffen collection, L.S.E.

Correspondents

EDWARD ROBERT BULWER-LYTTON, Earl Lytton, two letters, 1869.
Bulwer-Lytton papers, Hertfordshire R.O.

JOHN ELLIOT CAIRNES, three letters, 1862–1873.
N.L.I., MS. 8944.

ARTHUR HUGH CLOUGH, three letters, 1852–1858.
Bodleian, MS. Eng. Lett. d177, d179, e75.

WILLIAM EWART GLADSTONE, several letters, 1859–1873.
B.M. Add. MSS. 44392–44440.

WILLIAM STANLEY JEVONS, two letters, 1866.
Jevons papers, Manchester J.R.U.L.

SIR ROBERT HARRY INGLIS PALGRAVE, five letters, 1873–1875.
King's College, Cambridge.

SIR ROBERT HARRY INGLIS PALGRAVE, nine letters, 1873–1875.
Bagehot papers.[2]

HENRY CRABB ROBINSON, six letters, 1849–1856.
Crabb Robinson papers, Dr Williams' Library, London.

Printed Material

The Works and Life of Walter Bagehot, ed. Mrs Russell Barrington, 10 vols. (London, 1915).

Love Letters of Walter Bagehot and Eliza Wilson, ed. Mrs Russell Barrington (London, 1933).

The Collected Works of Walter Bagehot, ed. Norman St John Stevas, 9 vols., in progress (London, 1965–).
Vols. 7 and 8 will contain his economic writings with introduction by R. S. Sayers.

Palgrave I 79; *DNB* I 865; Boase I 123; *ESS* II 384; *IESS* I 498.

Portraits: N.P.G. (A); see *Collected Works* (above).

ALEXANDER BARING, 1st BARON ASHBURTON, 1774–1848

The business records of Baring Bros. include various papers relating to Alexander Baring's connection with the firm. In particular, the House Correspondence has in H.C. 1.20.1, 20 letters, 1828–1848, addressed by him to the firm on various matters.
Baring Bros. Archives.[14]

The papers of Sir Francis Baring (in the Northbrook papers) include some memoranda and letters of Alexander Baring.
Baring Bros. Archives.[14]

Documents and letters in various collections on both personal and business (mainly administration of lands owned by him) matters. Main correspondents: John Hare Powel, Thomas Cadwalader, 1796–1848.
Historical Society of Pennsylvania, Philadelphia.

Many letters from Baring and from Baring Bros.
Oliver papers, Maryland Historical Society, Baltimore.

The manuscripts of the Marquess of Northampton (at present on loan to Baring Bros.) include various papers connected with Alexander Baring.

Correspondents

HENRY PETER BROUGHAM, 1st Baron Brougham and Vaux, 15 letters, 1812–1847.
Brougham papers, U.C.L.

WILLIAM EWART GLADSTONE, three letters, 1843.
B.M. Add. MS. 44360.

GEORGE HAMILTON GORDON, 4th Earl of Aberdeen, 200 items (letters and memoranda), 1829–1846.
B.M. Add. MS. 43123.

ROBERT BANKS JENKINSON, 2nd Earl of Liverpool, three letters, 1818–1823.
B.M. Add. MSS. 38272–38297.

SIR JOHN NEWPORT, three letters, 1835–1840.
Newport MSS., Queen's University of Belfast.

DAVID PARISH, eight letters, 1807.
Parish papers, St Lawrence U.L., New York.

SIR ROBERT PEEL, 40 items of correspondence with many enclosures, 1834–1847.
B.M. Add. MSS. 40404–40598.

HENRY JOHN TEMPLE, 3rd Viscount Palmerston, two letters, 1843.
Broadlands papers, N.R.A. 12889.

DANIEL WEBSTER, two letters, 1842.
Webster papers, Library of Congress.

DANIEL WEBSTER, three letters, 1839.
Houghton Library, Harvard University.

SAMUEL WILBERFORCE, six letters, 1841–1844.
Bodleian, MSS. Wilberforce c7, c8, d17.

Printed Material

Papers Relative to the Special Mission of Lord Ashburton to the United States of America in 1842 (Shannon, Ireland, 1969).

DNB I 1110; *ESS* II 267.

Portrait: N.P.G.(A).

SIR FRANCIS BARING, 1740–1810

Business papers, including correspondence, accounts and memoranda, 1762–1810, relating to financial interests in Europe, South America and India. Political material, 1775–*c.* 1809, contained in boxes A, B and D of the Northbrook papers.
Baring Bros. Archives.[14]

Correspondence with various persons on East India Company matters, 1785–1807.
Home Miscellaneous Papers, India Office Library.

Answers to a series of questions on the East India Company's estimated sales and costs, *c.* 1792.
Manchester J.R.U.L., MS. 933

Correspondents

HENRY DUNDAS, 1st Viscount Melville, several letters, 1789–1808.
N.L.S., MS. 1064.

HENRY DUNDAS, 1st Viscount Melville, two letters, 1794–1807.
Melville Castle Muniments, Scottish R.O.

CHARLES GREY, 2nd Earl Grey, four letters, 1806.
Grey of Howick papers, Durham D.P.

ROBERT HOBART, 4th Earl of Buckinghamshire, several letters, 1794–1798.
MSS. of the Earl of Buckinghamshire, N.R.A. 0001.

CHARLES JENKINSON, 1st Earl of Liverpool, five letters, 1791–1793.
B.M. Add. MSS. 38228–38310.

GEORGE MACARTNEY, Earl Macartney, one or two letters, 1781–1785.
Macartney papers, University of Pennsylvania Libraries, Philadelphia.

WILLIAM PITT the Younger, four letters, n.d.
Chatham papers, P.R.O.

Printed Material
Palgrave I 121; *DNB* I 1112.

Portrait: Baring Bros.

JOHN BARTON, 1789–1852

A volume containing notes on economic conditions, and copies of his letters to the press.
Barton papers, L.S.E.

Correspondents
THOMAS CHALMERS, one letter, 1822.
Chalmers papers, St Andrews U.L.

CHARLES LENNOX, 5th Duke of Richmond, seven letters, 1831–1836.
Goodwood MSS., West Sussex R.O.

JEAN CHARLES LÉONARD SIMONDE DE SISMONDI, one letter, 1822.
Archivio Sismondi, Biblioteca Communale Pescia, Italy.

JOHN STRANG, one letter, 1826.
Records of the Dilettante Society of Glasgow, Glasgow City Archives.

SIR ROBERT JOHN WILMOT-HORTON, two letters, 1830.
Catton collection, Derby Borough Library.

Printed Material

JOHN BARTON, *Economic Writings*, ed. G. Sotiroff, 2 vols. (Regina, Saskatchewan, 1962–1963).

Palgrave I 122; *ESS* II 472.

Portrait: B.M.(P).

CHARLES FRANCIS BASTABLE, 1855–1945

After his death, Bastable's library was placed at the disposal of the School of Economics, Trinity College, Dublin. His papers do not seem to have been included with this. Since then a small group of about a dozen letters to him, and some printed papers, have been deposited in the Library of Trinity College.

Correspondents

EDWIN CANNAN, six letters, 1904.
Cannan collection, L.S.E.

SIR ROBERT GIFFEN, four letters, 1903–1906.
Giffen collection, L.S.E.

JOHN KELLS INGRAM, one letter, 1885.
Ingram papers, P.R.O.N.I.

EDWIN ROBERT ANDERSON SELIGMAN, 13 letters, 1887–1896.
Seligman papers, Columbia U.L., New York.

LÉON WALRAS, five letters, 1885–1890.
Fonds Walras, Bibliothèque Cantonale et Universitaire, Lausanne.

Printed Material

G. A. DUNCAN, 'Charles Francis Bastable, 1855–1945', *Proceedings of the British Academy*, XXXI (1945).

R. D. COLLISON BLACK, 'A Select Bibliography of Economic Writings by Members of Trinity College, Dublin', *Hermathena*, LXVI (1945) 62–65.

Includes a full bibliography of Bastable's writings.

Portrait: see Duncan (above); and *Centenary History of the Statistical and Social Inquiry Society of Ireland*, ed. R. D. Collison Black (Dublin, 1947).

JEREMY BENTHAM, 1748–1832

176 boxes of manuscript (and some printed) material, consisting of drafts of published and unpublished works, memoranda, notes and some of Bentham's correspondence, including that of his assistants.
Bentham MSS., U.C.L.

Correspondence and papers of the Bentham family. Ten bound volumes of the correspondence are Jeremy's and include the letters exchanged with his brother Samuel. Five volumes are manuscripts of his works, with tour journals and other papers.
B.M. Add. MSS. 33537–33564.

Bentham's notes on religion.
B.M. Add. MSS. 29806–29809.

A small collection of 15 of his letters to various correspondents, 1768–1830, two letters to him, and three fragments of manuscripts of his work.
King's College, Cambridge.

Printed Material

The Collected Works of Jeremy Bentham, ed. J. H. Burns (London, 1968–).

This edition, in an estimated 38 volumes, will collect Bentham's writings from both his manuscripts and his published works. Three volumes of correspondence have already been issued and the information for further volumes making up a complete correspondence is being collected by the Bentham Project at University College, London.

Jeremy Bentham's Economic Writings, ed. Werner Stark, 3 vols. (London, 1952–1954).

A compilation of his work on economics from manuscripts and published works.

ALEXANDER TAYLOR MILNE, *Catalogue of the Manuscripts of Jeremy Bentham in the Library of University College* (London, 1937).
Palgrave I 131; *DNB* II 268; *ESS* II 518; *IESS* II 55.
Portraits: B.M.(P); N.P.G.; Queen's College, Oxford; U.C.L.

JAMES BONAR, 1852–1941

A collection of letters and accounts relating to the Customs and shipping of Scotland while Adam Smith was Commissioner, 1765–1792. Collected by Bonar, and with his index.
Glasgow U.L.

Four volumes of notes taken from Edward Caird's lectures on moral philosophy, 1870–1871.
Glasgow U.L.

An unpublished, and unfinished, manuscript of a life of Malthus.
University of Illinois Library, Urbana.

Manuscript account of the origins of the Royal Statistical Society, written in 1930, and 17 pages long.
L.S.E.

Correspondents

WILLIAM HENRY BEVERIDGE, Baron Beveridge, a few letters, 1914–1937.
Beveridge papers, L.S.E.

EDWIN CANNAN, 60 letters, 1914–1932.
Cannan collection, L.S.E.

MRS G. M. GOULD, five letters, 1923–1928.
Gould papers, National Library of Medicine, Bethesda, Maryland.

JOHN MAYNARD KEYNES, Baron Keynes, 29 letters and 12 replies, 1913–1937.
Keynes papers, Marshall Library, Cambridge.

JOHN NEVILLE KEYNES, six letters, 1891–1907.
J. N. Keynes correspondence, Marshall Library, Cambridge.

WILLIAM R. SCOTT, nine letters, 1931–1939.
Scott papers, Glasgow U.L.

WILLIAM R. SCOTT, one letter, 1930.
Scott papers, P.R.O.N.I.

EDWIN ROBERT ANDERSON SELIGMAN, five letters, 1891–1910.
Seligman papers, Columbia U.L., New York.

HENRY SIDGWICK, two letters, 1893–1900.
Sidgwick papers, Trinity College, Cambridge.

HOMER VANDERBLUE, four letters, 1936–1939.
Foxwell papers, Baker Library, Harvard University

Printed Material

GEORGE FINDLAY SHIRRAS, 'James Bonar', *Proceedings of the British Academy*, xxviii (1942).

DNB 1941–1950, 90–1.

Portrait: see Shirras (above).

SIR ARTHUR LYON BOWLEY, 1869–1957

An unpublished lecture on socialism, *c.* 1896, with related correspondence between Bowley and R. F. George, 1953. 15 letters to Bowley from various correspondents, 1895–1935, and a few newspaper cuttings.
Bowley papers, Royal Statistical Society.[19]

Correspondents

WILLIAM HENRY BEVERIDGE, Baron Beveridge, several letters, 1920–1944.
Beveridge papers, L.S.E.

EDWIN CANNAN, 20 letters, 1906–1932.
Cannan collection, L.S.E.

JOHN MAYNARD KEYNES, Baron Keynes, 36 items, 1922–1944.
Keynes papers, Marshall Library, Cambridge.

SIR D'ARCY WENTWORTH THOMPSON, 18 letters, 1904–1938.
Thompson papers, St Andrews U.L.

GRAHAM WALLAS, two letters, 1909–1920.
Wallas papers, L.S.E.

Printed Material

AGATHA HILLIAM BOWLEY, *A Memoir of Professor Sir Arthur Bowley (1869–1957) and his Family* (1972).

IESS II 134.

Portrait: see Bowley (above).

JOHN FRANCIS BRAY, 1809–1897

One manuscript letter and several drafts of published and unpublished works, with photostats of letters, articles and other material.
Bray collection, L.S.E.

MS. of *God and Man a Unity*, written 1877–1878, and correspondence of 1883 about its publication. 'Log-books' from 1842–1896.
Seligman collection, Columbia U.L., New York.

Family letters, 1894 onwards, and manuscripts of unpublished works.
Labadie collection of Labor and Radical Literature, University of Michigan, Ann Arbor.

Family correspondence, 1802–1856, including several letters to Bray, 1824–1842, from his brothers and sisters, and some of his letters to his mother, aunt and uncle, 1822–1856.
Brotherton collection, Leeds U.L.

Printed Material

M. F. JOLLIFFE, 'John Francis Bray', *International Review for Social History*, IV (1939) 1–36.

JOHN FRANCIS BRAY, *A Voyage from Utopia*, ed. M. F. Lloyd-Prichard (London, 1957).

Palgrave I 177; *ESS* II 686.

Portrait: see *Voyage from Utopia* (above).

EDMUND BURKE, 1729–1797

Between 2000 and 3000 letters to and from Burke, in a chronological sequence, 1744–1797, along with much associated correspondence. Notes on French, American and Irish affairs. Papers on a variety of political questions, and many other miscellaneous papers. Correspondence and other papers of his executors.
Wentworth Woodhouse Muniments, Sheffield City Libraries.

Two groups of letters to Burke, one from English correspondents and one from French. Other correspondence, some being of members of his family. Bundles of notes and drafts of speeches on various topics, and other miscellaneous bundles including verses. 38 bundles in all, *c.* 1760–1795.
Fitzwilliam MSS., Northamptonshire R.O.

Printed Material

THOMAS W. COPELAND and MILTON S. SMITH, *A Checklist of the Correspondence of Edmund Burke* (Cambridge, 1955).

The Correspondence of Edmund Burke, ed. Thomas W. Copeland and John A. Woods, 9 vols. (London and Chicago, 1958–1970).

Includes the complete correspondence of Burke, from 1744–1797.

Palgrave I 194; *DNB* III 345; *ESS* III 74; *IESS* II 221.

Portrait: B.M.(P); N.P.G.

ISAAC BUTT, 1813–1879

Butt's correspondence, mainly on Home Rule, with some other papers.
N.L.I., MSS. 8686–8713, 10415, 13257.

Notes and original papers collected for a life of Butt.
N.L.I., MSS. 830–832, 12167–12168, 13150–13151.

A letter book of the Home Rule League, containing many letters from Butt to various correspondents, 1873–1878.
P.R.O.N.I.

Two Latin orations, 1834.
Trinity College, Dublin.

Correspondents

WILLIAM JOSEPH O'NEILL DAUNT, seven letters, 1873–1874.
N.L.I., MS. 10507.

GEORGE DELANEY, 19 letters, 1876–1879.
N.L.I., MS. 10512.

BENJAMIN DISRAELI, Earl of Beaconsfield, 13 letters, 1848–1851.
Disraeli papers, N.R.A. 0842.

WILLIAM EWART GLADSTONE, nine letters, 1834–1877.
B.M. Add. MSS. 44354–44455.

SIR MICHAEL HICKS-BEACH, 16 letters, 1876–1879.
St Aldwyn papers, Gloucestershire R.O.

SIR STAFFORD NORTHCOTE, three letters, 1878–1879.
B.M. Add. MS. 50040.

HENRY JOHN TEMPLE, 3rd Viscount Palmerston, three letters, 1857–1862.
Broadlands papers, N.R.A. 12889.

Printed Material

TERENCE DE VERE WHITE, *The Road of Excess* (Dublin, 1946).

DAVID THORNELY, *Isaac Butt and Home Rule* (London, 1964).

DNB III 545; Boase I 502; *ESS* III 126.

Portraits: see Thornely and White (above).

JOHN ELLIOT CAIRNES, 1823–1875

Personal papers, consisting of letters received, copies of letters sent, manuscripts of lectures and notes on economic topics, 1837–1875.
N.L.I., MSS. 8940–8986.

Letters from John Stuart Mill to Cairnes, 1858–1873, and notes made by Cairnes in 1864 on Mill's *Principles of Political Economy*.
Mill–Taylor collection, L.S.E.

Some correspondence concerning his position as Professor of Political Economy at University College, London.
College correspondence, U.C.L.

Correspondents

EDWIN CHADWICK, four letters, 1870–1871.
Chadwick papers, U.C.L.

LEONARD HENRY COURTNEY, 1st Baron Courtney of Penwith, 53 letters, 1862–1869.
Courtney collection, L.S.E.

GEORGE HOWELL, two letters, 1866–1870.
Howell papers, Bishopsgate Institute, London.

WILLIAM STANLEY JEVONS, six letters, 1863–1875.
Jevons papers, Manchester J.R.U.L.

HARRIET MARTINEAU, three letters, 1862.
Martineau papers, Birmingham U.L.

JOHN STUART MILL, letter or letters, n.d.
Mill papers, Yale U.L.

GEORGE CROOM ROBERTSON, six letters, 1867–1877.
Robertson papers, U.C.L.

SARAH BLAKE SHAW, 15 letters, 1862–1868.
Houghton Library, Harvard University.

HELEN TAYLOR, three letters, 1873–1875.
Mill–Taylor collection, L.S.E.

Printed Material

ADELAIDE WEINBERG, *John Elliot Cairnes and the American Civil War* (London, 1970).

Collected Works of John Stuart Mill, ed. J. M. Robson, VOL. III (Toronto, 1965) 1038–1095.
Includes Cairnes's letters to Mill.

Palgrave I 201; *DNB* III 668; Boase I 511; *ESS* III 140; *IESS* II 257.

Portrait: see *Centenary History of the Statistical and Social Inquiry Society of Ireland*, ed. R. D. Collison Black (Dublin, 1947).

EDWIN CANNAN, 1861–1935

Manuscript, typescript and printed papers in 143 volumes, 1876–1935, including correspondence, publishers' agreements and accounts, and other papers.
Cannan collection, L.S.E.

Correspondents

WILLIAM HENRY BEVERIDGE, Baron Beveridge, several letters, 1921–1934.
Beveridge papers, L.S.E.

C. F. BICKERDIKE, *c.* 20 letters, 1902–1924.
Bickerdike papers. [3]

JOHN MAYNARD KEYNES, Baron Keynes, 26 letters, 1912–1935.
Keynes papers, Marshall Library, Cambridge.

EDWIN ROBERT ANDERSON SELIGMAN, two letters, 1897–1930.
Seligman papers, Columbia U.L., New York.

GRAHAM WALLAS, three letters, 1914–1922.
Wallas papers, L.S.E.

Printed Material

EDWIN CANNAN, *An Economist's Protest* (London, 1927).

DNB 1931–1940, 141.

Portrait: see T. E. Gregory and Hugh Dalton, *London Essays in Economics* (London, 1927).

THOMAS CHALMERS, 1780–1847

Correspondence in 34 bound volumes, 1816–1847. Boxes of unbound correspondence on church, family and other matters. 15 volumes of copy letters. 20 volumes of journal, 1803–1844. 12 boxes of manuscripts of speeches, books, sermons and lectures, with notebooks.
Chalmers papers, New College, Edinburgh.

A bound volume of 439 letters to Chalmers, in alphabetical order of correspondents A–I, 1810–1825. Over 50 letters from Chalmers to various correspondents, 1813–1847.
St Andrews U.L.

Papers connected with his administrative work in the university, including Political Economy class lists.
St Andrews University Archives.

Notes from his lectures on theology.
Edinburgh U.L.

Notes on some of his sermons, taken by Charles Hutcheson.
N.L.S., MS. 2773.

Three volumes of notes from his lectures on theology.
U.C.L.

11 letters to various correspondents, 1808–1838.
Foxwell collection, Baker Library, Harvard University.

Four letters to various correspondents, 1832–1841.
Houghton Library, Harvard University.

Correspondents

HENRY PETER BROUGHAM, 1st Baron Brougham and Vaux, seven letters, 1826–1846.
Brougham papers, U.C.L.

JAMES BROWN, 27 letters, 1798–1836.
Edinburgh U.L.

WILLIAM BUCHANAN, 43 letters, 1820–1847.
Glasgow U.L.

ARCHIBALD CONSTABLE, many letters, 1802–1818.
N.L.S., MS. 669.

GEORGE HAMILTON GORDON, 4th Earl of Aberdeen, ten items, 1835–1842.
B.M. Add. MSS. 43237, 43240.

J. Hope, four letters, 1835.
B.M. Add. MS. 43202.

SIR JAMES PHILLIPS KAY-SHUTTLEWORTH, five letters, 1833–1834.
Kay-Shuttleworth MSS., Manchester J.R.U.L.

JOHN LEE, 24 letters, 1822–1843.
N.L.S., Lee papers.

ROBERT LUNDIE, six letters, 1816–1840.
N.L.S., MS. 1676.

SIR JAMES MACKINTOSH, two letters, 1829.
B.M. Add. MS. 52453.

THOMAS ROBERT MALTHUS, one letter, 1821.
N.L.S., MS. 3112.

MACVEY NAPIER, four letters, 1829–1837.
B.M. Add. MSS. 34614–34618.

ROBERT PAUL, five letters, 1817–1845.
N.L.S., MSS. 5139–5140.

SIR ROBERT PEEL, ten items, 1822–1843.
B.M. Add. MSS. 40351–40598.

JAMES REDDIE, four letters, 1818–1826.
N.L.S., MS. 3704.

SIR GEORGE SINCLAIR, *c.* 20 letters, 1823–1846.
Sinclair of Ulbster papers, N.R.A. 10552.

THOMAS SPRING-RICE, 1st Baron Monteagle, three letters, 1830–1837.
N.L.S., MS. 2225.

WILLIAM WHEWELL, four letters, 1834–1837.
Whewell papers, Trinity College, Cambridge.

SIR ROBERT JOHN WILMOT-HORTON, five letters (and a 13-page MS. signed by Chalmers), 1826–1830.
Catton collection, Derby Borough Library.

Printed Material

A Selection from the Correspondence of the Late Thomas Chalmers, ed. William Hanna (Edinburgh, 1853).

WILLIAM HANNA, *Memoirs of the Life and Writings of Thomas Chalmers*, 4 vols. (Edinburgh, 1849–1852).

The Correspondence between Dr Chalmers and the Earl of Aberdeen in the Years 1839 and 1840 (Edinburgh, 1893).

Palgrave I 255; *DNB* III 1358; *ESS* III 321.

Portrait: N.P.G. (A); S.N.P.G.

SIR SYDNEY JOHN CHAPMAN, 1871–1951

Typescript autobiography: 'Some Memories and Reflections'. (261 pp.).
Manchester J.R.U.L.

Another copy of the above.
L.S.E.

Printed Material
DNB 1951–60.

SIR JOHN HAROLD CLAPHAM, 1873–1946

A volume of notes and essays, 1894, 12 papers read to the King's College Political Society, eight letters to various correspondents, 1915–1946. The manuscript of his fellowship dissertation on the Abbé Sieyès. Two volumes of notes for lectures, one on France before the Revolution and the other on modern European economic history.
King's College, Cambridge.

A typescript copy, with numerous manuscript annotations, of *The Causes of the War of 1792*, 1898. Also a few manuscript fragments of the *Concise Economic History*.
Clapham papers.[4]

The manuscript of the unfinished third volume of the *History of the Bank of England*.
Bank of England, Archives Section.

Correspondents
WILLIAM HENRY BEVERIDGE, Baron Beveridge, several letters, 1926–1941.
Beveridge papers, L.S.E.

EDWIN CANNAN, 11 letters, 1911–1930.
Cannan collection, L.S.E.

CHARLES RYLE FAY, five letters, 1908.
Miscellaneous letters, Marshall Library, Cambridge.

MONTAGUE RHODES JAMES, 13 letters, n.d.
Cambridge U.L., Add. MS. 7481.

JOHN MAYNARD KEYNES, Baron Keynes, 35 letters, 1915–1946.
Keynes papers, Marshall Library, Cambridge.

JOHN SALTMARSH, 15 letters, 1930–1946.
Papers of Mr John Saltmarsh.[5]

FRANCIS WILLIAM TAUSSIG, two letters, n.d.
Harvard University Archives, Widener Library.

Printed Material

SIR GEORGE N. CLARK, 'Sir John Harold Clapham, 1873–1946', *Proceedings of the British Academy*, XXXIII (1947).

DNB 1941–1950, 153–5; *IESS* II 502.

Portrait: see Clark (above).

WILLIAM COBBETT, 1762–1835

About 300 family letters, 1791–1833, including many to and from Cobbett (particularly with his daughter Anne). A few miscellaneous notes for lectures or articles, and some biographical notes on Cobbett himself.
Cobbett papers, Nuffield College, Oxford.

Some letters and memoranda, 1831–1838. Two manuscripts, 1830 and 1831. Correspondence concerning the *Weekly Register*, 1800–1810.
B.M. Add. MSS. 31125, 31857, 22906, 22907.

A small collection of papers, including accounts, lecture notes and letters to J. Y. Akerman and Joseph Bradley.
Fitzwilliam Museum, Cambridge.

A collection of Cobbett's letters to various correspondents, including Messrs Bagshaw, Dean, Gutsell, Oldfield, Wright and

Dr French Laurence, 1797–1835.
Cobbett collection, University of Illinois Library, Urbana.

An account book relating to his bookselling activities in Philadelphia, 1796–1800.
American Antiquarian Society, Philadelphia.

Ten letters to various correspondents, 1800–1835.
Rutgers U.L., New Jersey.

Two manuscripts of editions of *Cobbett's Weekly Political Register*, 1822 and 1828, with letters to various correspondents, 1802–1834.
Houghton Library, Harvard University.

Various collections include letters of Cobbett to different correspondents, 1793–1832.
Pennsylvania Historical Society, Philadelphia.

Correspondents

JAMES PAUL COBBETT, copies of letters (with some to other correspondents), 1820–1827.
B.M. Add. MS. 31127.

JAMES MATHIEU, 23 letters, 1793.
Pennsylvania Historical Society, Philadelphia.

GEORGE O'BRIEN, 3rd Earl of Egremont, three letters, 1821.
Petworth House Archives, N.R.A. 15719.

WILLIAM WINDHAM, over 200 items, 1800–1806.
B.M. Add. MS. 37853.

JOHN WRIGHT, many letters, 1807–1810.
B.M. Add. MS. 31126.

Printed Material

LEWIS MELVILLE, *Life and Letters of William Cobbett* (London, 1913).

GEORGE DOUGLAS HOWARD COLE, *The Life of William Cobbett* (London, 1924).

Palgrave I 314; *DNB* IV 598; *ESS* III 602.

Portrait: B.M. (P); N.P.G.

RICHARD COBDEN, 1804–1865

Correspondence, 1836–1865, diaries, 1836–1861, and a few other papers.
B.M. Add. MSS. 43647–43678, 43807–43808, 50131, 50748–50751.

Correspondence, 1832–1865, including many copies of out-letters. Accounts, both business and estate, papers and notes on various topics, diaries and journals.
Cobden papers, West Sussex R.O.

Some correspondence and a few miscellaneous papers, 1815–1865.
Cobden–Sanderson collection, West Sussex R.O.

A small amount of correspondence, 1836–1861.
Cobden and Unwin papers, West Sussex R.O.

Cobden family papers, including some letters to and from Richard Cobden, mainly on business matters, 1825–1857.
Manchester City Library.

Letters addressed to Cobden on the business of the Anti-Corn Law League are in the letter books of the League, 1838–1840.
Manchester City Library.

Eight letters to various correspondents, 1842–1863.
London U.L., A.L.s 33–38, 351, 250.

Nine letters to various correspondents, 1841–1855, in various collections.
Henry E. Huntington Library, San Marino, California.

Correspondents

EDWARD BAINES, ten letters, 1841–1855.
Baines papers, Leeds City Library, Archives Dept.

JOHN BRIGHT, both sides of the correspondence, 1837–1865.
B.M. Add. MSS. 43383–43384, 43649–43652.

HENRY PETER BROUGHAM, 1st Baron Brougham and Vaux, nine letters, 1838–1863.
Brougham papers, U.C.L.

JOHN HILL BURTON, *c.* 20 letters, 1839–1846.
N.L.S., MS. 9406.

HENRY CATT, three letters, 1861.
University of Chicago Library.

EDWARD DAVIES DAVENPORT, five letters, 1843–1845.
Bromley-Davenport Muniments, Manchester J.R.U.L.

THOMAS HAINES DUDLEY, four letters, 1863–1864.
Henry E. Huntington Library, San Marino, California.

WILLIAM EWART GLADSTONE, over 400 letters, 1841–1865.
B.M. Add. MSS. 44135–44136.

ALEXANDER IRELAND, *c.* 12 letters, 1855–1865.
B.M. Add. MS. 33515.

SIR LOUIS MALLET, 66 letters, 1860–1865.
Mallet papers.[6]

JOSEPH PARKES, seven items, 1852–1861.
Parkes papers, U.C.L.

FRANCIS PLACE, seven items, 1840–1846.
B.M. Add. MS. 35151.

JAMES EDWIN THOROLD ROGERS, 55 items, 1854–1865.
Thorold Rogers papers, N.R.A. 12396.

LORD JOHN RUSSELL, 1st Earl Russell, *c.* 12 letters, 1852–1860.
B.M. Add. MS. 38080.

SAMUEL SMILES, 15 letters, 1841–1863.
Fitzwilliam Museum, Cambridge.

JOHN BENJAMIN SMITH, 115 letters, 1839–1865.
J. B. Smith papers, Manchester City Library.

THOMAS SPENCER, four letters, 1848–1849.
Spencer papers, London U.L., MS. 791.

JOSEPH STURGE, many letters, 1839–1859.
B.M. Add. MSS. 43722, 50131.

HENRY JOHN TEMPLE, 3rd Viscount Palmerston, four letters, 1859–1860.
Broadlands papers, N.R.A. 12889.

THOMAS THOMASSON, 22 letters, 1850–1864.
L.S.E.

GEORGE WILSON, *c.* 200 letters, 1837–1864.
George Wilson papers, Manchester City Library.

Printed Material

The American Diaries of Richard Cobden, ed. Elizabeth Hoon Cawley (Princeton, 1952).

EDWARD HUGHES, *The Development of Cobden's Economic Doctrines and his Methods of Propaganda: Some Unpublished Correspondence* (Manchester, 1938).

JOHN MORLEY, Viscount Morley of Blackburn, *Life of Richard Cobden* (London, 1881).

Palgrave I 316; *DNB* IV 604; Boase I 659; *ESS* III 602.

Portrait: B.M. (P); N.P.G.

SIR FREDERICK MORTON EDEN, BT, 1766–1809

A commonplace book, 1787–1802.
B.M. Add. MS. 43702.

Manuscript entitled 'Epsom: a Vision', 1797, 52 pages.
Houghton Library, Harvard University.

The minutes of the Committee of Insurance and the Treasury Committee of the Globe Insurance Company, 1803–1809, are signed by Eden as chairman. A report on remuneration of firemen to the Committee of Insurance, pp. 133–135, is a rare example of his personal contribution being recorded.
Guildhall Library, MSS. 11657–11658.

Correspondents

JEREMY BENTHAM, four letters, 1797–1803.
B.M. Add. MSS. 33542–33544.

JONATHAN BOUCHER, 30 items, 1786–1800.
Boucher papers, East Sussex R.O.

WILLIAM EDEN, 1st Baron Auckland, four letters, 1798–1806.
B.M. Add. MSS. 34454–34457.

ROYAL SOCIETY OF ARTS, one letter, 1797.
Royal Society of Arts Library, London.

NICHOLAS VANSITTART, Baron Bexley, one letter (with comments by Jeremy Bentham), 1807.
B.M. Add. MS. 31235.

Printed Material

Catalogue [of the Library of Sir F. M. Eden, Compiled by Himself] (1806).

Palgrave I 679; *DNB* VI 356; *ESS* V 397.

FRANCIS YSIDRO EDGEWORTH, 1845–1926

Letters to Edgeworth, 1875–1916, mainly testimonials and congratulations. These include many from economists, but none which have significant material on economics. Offprints of reviews of works on economics, mainly from the *Academy*. Printed applications for university posts. A few newspaper cuttings relating to papers given by Edgeworth.
Edgeworth papers.[7]

Correspondents

C. F. BICKERDIKE, *c.* 50 letters, 1902–1906.
Bickerdike papers.[3]

EDWIN CANNAN, 18 letters, 1906–1925.
Cannan collection, L.S.E.

SIR ROBERT ENSOR, two letters, 1899–1900.
Ensor papers, Corpus Christi College, Oxford.

HERBERT SOMERTON FOXWELL, four letters, 1899.
Foxwell papers, Baker Library, Harvard University.

JOHN MAYNARD KEYNES, Baron Keynes, 72 items, 1908–1925.
Keynes papers, Marshall Library, Cambridge.

JOHN NEVILLE KEYNES, nine letters, 1890–1900.
J. N. Keynes correspondence, Marshall Library, Cambridge.

EDWIN ROBERT ANDERSON SELIGMAN, 43 letters, 1891–1916.
Seligman papers, Columbia U.L., New York.

LÉON WALRAS, ten letters, 1888–1890.
Fonds Walras, Bibliothèque Cantonale et Universitaire, Lausanne.

KNUT WICKSELL, eight letters, 1894–1915.
Wicksell papers, Lund Universitetsbibliotek, Sweden.

Printed Material

ARTHUR LYON BOWLEY, *F. Y. Edgeworth's Contribution to Mathematical Statistics* (London, 1928).

JOHN MAYNARD KEYNES, 'Francis Ysidro Edgeworth', in *Essays in Biography*, vol. X of *Collected Writings* (London, 1972).

JAMES BONAR, 'Memories of F. Y. Edgeworth', *Economic Journal*, XXXVI (1926) 647–653.

DNB 1922–1930, 284; *ESS* V 397; *IESS* IV 506.

Portraits: see Keynes and Bonar (above).

WILLIAM ELLIS, 1800–1881

Ellis's personal papers are recorded as having been destroyed (see Ellis and Blyth, below).

Records of his professional career with the Indemnity Marine Insurance Company, in the form of financial reports and correspondence on behalf of the company.
Guildhall Library, MSS. 11831–11890.

Correspondents

HENRY PETER BROUGHAM, 1st Baron Brougham and Vaux, eight letters, 1848–1860.
Brougham papers, U.C.L.

EDWIN CHADWICK, three letters, 1841–1865.
Chadwick papers, U.C.L.

GEORGE COMBE, several hundred letters with replies, 1846–1858.
N.L.S., Combe papers.

Printed Material

ETHEL ELLIS, *Memoirs of William Ellis* (London, 1888).

EDMUND KELL BLYTH, *Life of William Ellis* (London, 1889).

Palgrave I 693; *DNB* VI 716; Boase I 986.

Portrait: see Blyth (above).

HENRY FAWCETT, 1833–1884

His papers are not held by the Fawcett family, the Fawcett Library or Trinity Hall, Cambridge.

41 letters from John Stuart Mill, 1860–1870, and one letter from W. T. Thornton, 1862.
Mill–Taylor collection, L.S.E.

Correspondents

HENRY PETER BROUGHAM, 1st Baron Brougham and Vaux, four letters, 1860–1861.
Brougham papers, U.C.L.

EDWIN CHADWICK, five letters, 1874–1880.
Chadwick papers, U.C.L.

SIR CHARLES DILKE, ten letters, 1868–1880.
B.M. Add. MSS. 43909–43910.

WILLIAM EWART GLADSTONE, many letters, 1865–1884.
B.M. Add. MS. 44156.

FANNY HERTZ, eight letters, 1859–1864.
Miscellaneous letters, Marshall Library, Cambridge.

GEORGE JACOB HOLYOAKE, four letters, 1865–1878.
Holyoake collection, Co-operative Union Ltd, Manchester.

GEORGE HOWELL, eight letters, 1866–1884.
Howell papers, Bishopsgate Institute, London.

JOHN NEVILLE KEYNES, eight letters, 1875–1884.
Cambridge U.L., Add. MS. 7562.

MACMILLANS, several letters, 1872–1879.
B.M. Add. MS. 55206.

JOHN STUART MILL, letter or letters, n.d.
Mill papers, Yale U.L.

CHARLES HENRY PEARSON, three letters, 1879–1883.
Bodleian, MS. Eng. Lett. d187.

JAMES EDWIN THOROLD ROGERS, four letters, 1862–1884.
Thorold Rogers papers, N.R.A. 12396.

SEDLEY TAYLOR, 17 letters, 1873–1884.
Cambridge U.L., Add. MS. 6258.

Printed Material

LESLIE STEPHEN, *Life of Henry Fawcett* (London, 1885).

Palgrave II 41; *DNB* VI 1125; Boase I 1027; *ESS* VI 153.

Portraits: N.P.G.; Fitzwilliam Museum, Cambridge.

ADAM FERGUSON, 1723–1818

32 essays on philosophical topics with a few fragments of notes. Three volumes of lectures on pneumatics and moral philosophy (mainly 1776–1785). A copy of the Proceedings of the British Commissioners at Philadelphia, 1778–1779, partly in Ferguson's hand.
Edinburgh U.L.

Many single letters by Ferguson to various correspondents are in collections at the National Library of Scotland, Edinburgh U.L., Glasgow U.L.

Correspondents

ALEXANDER CARLYLE, 17 letters, 1775–1802.
Edinburgh U.L.

ALEXANDER CARLYLE, copies of letters, and other material, 1775–1800.
N.L.S., Lee papers.

HENRY DUNDAS, 1st Viscount Melville, two letters, 1780 and 1810.
Melville Castle Muniments, Scottish R.O.

SIR JOHN MACPHERSON, 72 letters, 1773–1808.
Edinburgh U.L.

CHRISTOPHER WYVILL, one or two letters, 1782.
Wyvill papers, North Riding R.O.

Printed Material

ADAM FERGUSON, *Saggio sulla Storia della Società Civile*, ed. Pasquale Salvucci (Florence, 1973).
Includes an excellent bibliography and list of manuscripts.

DAVID KETTLER, *The Social and Political Thought of Adam Ferguson* (Columbus, Ohio, 1965).

JOHN SMALL, *Biographical Sketch of Adam Ferguson* (Edinburgh, 1864).

Palgrave II 53; *DNB* VI 1200; *ESS* VI 184; *IESS* V 369.

Portraits: B.M. (P); N.P.G. (A).

HERBERT SOMERTON FOXWELL, 1849–1936

Foxwell's papers, in great profusion and including a vast correspondence on economic, bibliographical, personal and other matters, are at present being sorted prior to the writing of a study on Foxwell and are unlikely to be available for a period of years. Details with N.R.A.

Letters of Foxwell to R. A. Rye, the Goldsmith's Librarian, and other officials of London University, *c.* 100 items, 1903–1916.
Correspondence of Sir Walter Prideaux of the Goldsmith's Company including many letters from Foxwell, *c.* 330 items, 1900–1916.
London U.L., MSS. 789–790.

Some of Foxwell's correspondence, including *c.* 400 letters to him from various correspondents, and 72 letters to W. R. Scott, 1889–1933, and a few to James Bonar. Manuscripts of two lectures given to the City of London, 1894.
Foxwell papers, Baker Library, Harvard University.

Letters to C. C. Eaton, Arthur H. Cole and Wallace B. Donham, 35 in all, 1927–1932.
Baker Library Archives, Harvard University.

Correspondence and printed testimonials relating to his appointment as Professor at University College, London, 1881. College correspondence, U.C.L.

Correspondents

H. R. BEETON, three letters, 1894.
Miscellaneous letters, Marshall Library, Cambridge.

SIR ARTHUR LYON BOWLEY, two letters, 1901–1906.
Bowley papers, Royal Statistical Society.[19]

EDWIN CANNAN, 16 letters, 1893–1929.
Cannan collection, L.S.E.

CLARA COLLET, three letters, 1908.
Collet papers.[8]

SIR GEORGE DARWIN, four letters, 1901–1903.
Miscellaneous letters, Marshall Library, Cambridge.

FRANCIS YSIDRO EDGEWORTH, three letters, 1881–1888.
Edgeworth papers.[7]

CHARLES RYLE FAY, eight letters, 1908–1926.
Miscellaneous letters, Marshall Library, Cambridge.

GEORGE HOWELL, 11 letters, 1892–1906.
Howell papers, Bishopsgate Institute, London.

FRANCIS JOHN HENRY JENKINSON, 23 letters, 1889–1922.
Cambridge U.L., Add. MS. 6463.

WILLIAM STANLEY JEVONS, two letters, 1879–1882.
Jevons papers, Manchester J.R.U.L.

JOHN MAYNARD KEYNES, Baron Keynes, 23 letters, 1910–1932.
Keynes papers, Marshall Library, Cambridge.

JOHN NEVILLE KEYNES, 34 letters, 1877–1917.
J. N. Keynes correspondence, Marshall Library, Cambridge.

SIR JOSEPH LARMOR, 14 letters, 1893–1923.
St John's College, Cambridge.

MACMILLANS, many letters, 1885–1920.
B.M. Add. MS. 55196.

SIR ROBERT HARRY INGLIS PALGRAVE, 17 letters, 1885–1906.
Palgrave papers.[9]

EDWIN ROBERT ANDERSON SELIGMAN, 19 letters, 1888–1928.
Seligman papers, Columbia U.L., New York.

SEDLEY TAYLOR, three letters, 1884.
Cambridge U.L., Add. MS. 6258.

FRANCIS A. WALKER, eight letters, 1893–1896.
Walker papers, Library of Congress.

GRAHAM WALLAS, three letters, 1891–1898.
Wallas papers, L.S.E.

LÉON WALRAS, 22 letters, 1882–1893.
Fonds Walras, Bibliothèque Cantonale et Universitaire, Lausanne.

ALLYN YOUNG, three letters, 1928–1929.
Baker Library Archives, Harvard University.

Printed Material

JOHN MAYNARD KEYNES, 'Herbert Somerton Foxwell', *Proceedings of the British Academy*, XXIV (1938).

JOHN MAYNARD KEYNES, 'Herbert Somerton Foxwell', in *Essays in Biography*, vol. X of *Collected Writings* (London, 1972).

DNB 1931–1940, 293.

Portraits: N.P.G. (A); see Keynes (above).

SIR ROBERT GIFFEN, 1837–1910

Correspondence, 1861–1910, mainly on personal matters, but some on currency and other economic topics. Miscellaneous papers and newspaper cuttings, six volumes in all.
Giffen collection, L.S.E.

Correspondents

JOSEPH CHAMBERLAIN, six letters, 1881–1887.
Chamberlain papers, Birmingham U.L.

LORD RANDOLPH CHURCHILL, three items, 1886.
Churchill papers, Churchill College, Cambridge.

WILLIAM EWART GLADSTONE, nine letters and memoranda, 1879–1886.
B.M. Add. MSS. 44258–44666.

SIR MICHAEL HICKS-BEACH, several letters, 1889–1897.
St Aldwyn papers, Gloucestershire R.O.

SIR ROBERT HARRY INGLIS PALGRAVE, six letters, 1871–1894.
Palgrave papers.[9]

EDWIN ROBERT ANDERSON SELIGMAN, two letters, 1895.
Seligman papers, Columbia U.L., New York.

HERBERT SPENCER, two letters, 1885–1896.
Spencer papers, London U.L., MS. 791.

Printed Material
ESS VI 656; *IESS* VI 181.

Portrait: *Journal of the Royal Statistical Society* (May 1909).

GEORGE JOACHIM GOSCHEN, 1st VISCOUNT GOSCHEN, 1831–1907

A few papers of Goschen (which were originally part of the Balfour papers), including correspondence with A. J. Balfour and some letters on Oxford University matters.
Bodleian, MS. Dep. c182–c183.

A register of Goschen's letters as First Lord of the Admiralty, 1895–1900.
Bodleian, MS. Eng. Hist. c386.

Letters to and from Goschen on financial questions, 1887–1897, with one or two other papers.
Welby collection, L.S.E.

Correspondents
ARTHUR JAMES BALFOUR, 1st Earl of Balfour, many letters, 1887–1906.
B.M. Add. MS. 49706.

JOHN EDWARD COURTENAY BODLEY, five letters, 1884–1886.
Bodleian, MS. Eng. Lett. d174.

HENRY BROADHURST, three letters, 1890–1893.
Broadhurst collection, L.S.E.

EDWARD CARDWELL, correspondence and memoranda, 1869–1874.
Cardwell papers, P.R.O.

EDWIN CHADWICK, 11 letters, n.d.
Chadwick papers, U.C.L.

JOSEPH CHAMBERLAIN, 23 items, 1886–1899.
Chamberlain papers, Birmingham U.L.

LORD RANDOLPH CHURCHILL, 14 items, 1886–1893.
Churchill papers, Churchill College, Cambridge.

SIR RICHARD ASSHETON CROSS, 27 letters, 1882–1901.
B.M. Add. MS. 51267.

SIR CHARLES DILKE, about 15 items, 1878–1906.
B.M. Add. MSS. 43910–43919.

WILLIAM EWART GLADSTONE, many letters, 1865–1896.
B.M. Add. MS. 44161.

ALBERT HENRY GEORGE GREY, 4th Earl Grey, about 30 letters, n.d.
Grey of Howick papers, Durham D.P.

FREDERIC HARRISON, five letters, 1863–1869.
Harrison papers, L.S.E.

THOMAS HUGHES, two letters, 1886.
Bodleian, MS. Eng. Lett. e94.

GRANVILLE GEORGE LEVESON-GOWER, 2nd Earl Granville, several letters, 1868–1874.
Granville papers, P.R.O.

GEORGE MELLY, eight letters, 1867–1873.
Melly correspondence, Liverpool R.O.

FRIEDRICH MAX MÜLLER, three letters, 1887–1896.
Bodleian, MS. Dep. d170.

SIR STAFFORD NORTHCOTE, eight letters, 1876–1885.
B.M. Add. MS. 50021.

SIR ROBERT HARRY INGLIS PALGRAVE, 14 letters, 1873–1886.
Palgrave papers.[9]

CHARLES HENRY PEARSON, 16 letters, 1860–1893.
Bodleian, MS. Eng. Lett. d188.

GEORGE FREDERICK SAMUEL ROBINSON, 2nd Earl of Ripon, ten letters, 1866–1888.
B.M. Add. MS. 43532.

GEORGE WILLIAM FREDERICK VILLIERS, 4th Earl of Clarendon, a few letters, 1868–1870.
Bodleian, MS. Clar. Dep. c500.

SIR EDGAR VINCENT, Viscount D'Abernon, 36 letters, 1881–1900.
B.M. Add. MS. 48922.

REGINALD EARLE WELBY, 1st Baron Welby, several letters, 1888–1891.
B.M. Eg. MSS. 3291B and D.

CHARLES WOOD, 1st Viscount Halifax, ten letters, 1871–1884.
Hickleton papers, N.R.A. 8128.

Printed Material

PERCY COLSON, *Lord Goschen and his Friends* (London, 1946).

ARTHUR RALPH DOUGLAS ELLIOTT, *Life of Lord Goschen*, 2 vols. (London, 1911).

DNB 1901–1911, 134; *ESS* VI 705.

Portraits: N.P.G. (A); see Colson (above).

SIR JAMES ROBERT GEORGE GRAHAM, BT, 1792–1861

Political correspondence, *c.* 1820–1850, particularly concerning Home Office, Irish and Naval affairs.
Graham papers, N.R.A. 2634. (Microfilms of this collection in the Bodleian, Cambridge U.L., National Library of Ireland and the Newberry Library, Chicago.)

Correspondents

WILLIAM A'COURT, 1st Baron Heytesbury, copies of eight letters, 1845–1846.
Newcastle MSS., Nottingham U.L.

FRANCIS ROBERT BONHAM, many letters, 1837–1857.
B.M. Add. MS. 40616.

HENRY PETER BROUGHAM, 1st Baron Brougham and Vaux, 110 letters, 1818–1857.
Brougham papers, U.C.L.

SIR GEORGE BROWN, a few letters, 1843.
N.L.S., MS. 2843.

EDWARD CARDWELL, many letters, 1852–1859.
Cardwell papers, P.R.O.

EDWIN CHADWICK, 30 items, 1841–1851.
Chadwick papers, U.C.L.

HENRY PELHAM CLINTON, 5th Duke of Newcastle, 67 letters, 1840–1861.
Newcastle MSS., Nottingham U.L.

SIR THOMAS JOHN COCHRANE, 30 letters, 1840–1855.
N.L.S., MS. 2280 *et seq.*

JOHN SINGLETON COPLEY, Baron Lyndhurst, 14 letters, 1842–1844.
Copley papers, Glamorgan R.O.

BENJAMIN DISRAELI, Earl of Beaconsfield, three letters, 1842–1851.
Disraeli papers, N.R.A. 0842.

HENRY DUNCAN, several letters, 1834–1835.
Crawford papers, N.R.A. 12609.

ROBERT DUNDAS, 2nd Viscount Melville, eight items, 1831–1832.
Melville Castle Muniments, Scottish R.O.

HENRY RICHARD VASSALL FOX, 3rd Baron Holland (and Lady Holland), 55 letters, *c.* 1826–1840.
B.M. Add. MS. 51542.

WILLIAM EWART GLADSTONE, many letters, 1837–1855.
B.M. Add. MSS. 44163–44164.

GEORGE HAMILTON GORDON, 4th Earl of Aberdeen, many letters, 1840–1860.
B.M. Add. MSS. 43190–43192.

HENRY HARDINGE, 1st Viscount Hardinge, 20 letters, 1836–1854.
Hardinge papers, McGill University, Montreal.

GEORGE WILLIAM HOPE, several letters, 1841–1856.
Hope of Luffness papers, N.R.A. 10172.

JOHN GEORGE LAMBTON, 1st Earl of Durham, a few letters, n.d.
Lambton papers, N.R.A. 11184.

WILLIAM WALTER LEGGE, 5th Earl of Dartmouth, four letters, 1842–1854.
Dartmouth MSS., William Salt Library, Stafford.

SIR THOMAS MARTIN, many letters, 1830–1854.
B.M. Add. MSS. 41368–41466.

SIR CHARLES NAPIER, many letters, 1827–1854.
B.M. Add. MSS. 40023–40026, 40037.

JOSEPH PARKES, two letters, 1854.
Parkes papers, U.C.L.

SIR ROBERT PEEL, much correspondence, 1827–1850.
B.M. Add. MSS. 40318, 40446–40452.

SIR GEORGE SINCLAIR, several letters, 1835–1841.
Sinclair of Ulbster papers, N.R.A. 10552.

GEORGE JOHN SPENCER, 2nd Earl Spencer, nine letters, 1831–1833.
Spencer papers, N.R.A. 10410.

CHARLES WILLIAM STEWART, 3rd Marquess of Londonderry, 71 letters, 1841–1852.
Londonderry papers, Durham R.O.

HENRY JOHN TEMPLE, 3rd Viscount Palmerston, 80 letters, 1831–1861.
Broadlands papers, N.R.A. 12889.

GEORGE WILLIAM FREDERICK VILLIERS, 4th Earl of Clarendon, many letters, 1834–1855.
Bodleian, MS. Clar. Dep. c4, c14, c30, c469.

THOMAS WALLACE, Baron Wallace, three letters, 1813.
Middleton papers, Northumberland R.O.

SAMUEL WILBERFORCE, nine letters, 1837–1857.
Bodleian, MS. Wilberforce.

SIR ROBERT JOHN WILMOT-HORTON, two letters, 1831–1833.
Catton collection, Derby Borough Library.

CHARLES WOOD, 1st Viscount Halifax, 87 letters, 1846–1861.
Hickleton papers, N.R.A. 8128.

Printed Material

ARVEL B. ERICKSON, *The Public Career of Sir James Graham* (Oxford, 1952).

CHARLES STUART PARKER, *Life and Letters of Sir James Graham Baronet of Netherby, P.C., G.C.B., 1792–1861* (London, 1907).

JOHN T. WARD, *Sir James Graham* (London, 1967).

Palgrave II 249; *DNB* VIII 328; Boase I 1196.

Portraits: B.M. (P); N.P.G. (A); see Ward (above).

WILLIAM NEILSON HANCOCK, 1820–1888

Papers connected with his academic appointments.
State Paper Office (Dublin Castle), Official papers 1848, no. 144, Registered papers 1853, 9673.

Statistical returns signed by Hancock, but in another hand.
Abercorn papers, P.R.O.N.I.

Proof copy, with manuscript corrections, of a paper on the Land Question, 1869.
N.L.I., MS. 2268.

Correspondents

WILLIAM EWART GLADSTONE, letters and memoranda, 1869–1873.
B.M. Add. MS. 44421.

JOHN KELLS INGRAM, two letters, 1850–1888.
Ingram papers, P.R.O.N.I.

SIR THOMAS LARCOM, letters and memoranda, n.d.
Larcom papers, N.L.I.

JOHN STRANG, two letters, 1852–1856.
Records of the Dilettante Society of Glasgow, Glasgow City Archives.

Printed Material
Palgrave II 278; *ESS* VII 254.

Portrait: see *Centenary History of the Statistical and Social Inquiry Society of Ireland*, ed. R. D. Collison Black (Dublin, 1947).

SIR HUBERT DOUGLAS HENDERSON, 1890–1952

About 20 boxes of professional papers, consisting of memoranda, notes, reports, etc., with some correspondence. Mainly dating from 1931–1949.
Henderson papers, Nuffield College, Oxford.

Correspondents
WILLIAM HENRY BEVERIDGE, Baron Beveridge, several letters, 1922–1948.
Beveridge papers, L.S.E.

JOHN MAYNARD KEYNES, Baron Keynes, *c.* 100 items, 1914–1940.
Keynes papers, Marshall Library, Cambridge.

GRAHAM WALLAS, five letters, 1920–1926.
Wallas papers, L.S.E.

Printed Material
'Sir Hubert Henderson, 1890–1952', ed. T. Wilson, *Oxford Economic Papers*, supplement (June 1953).

DNB 1951–1960, 470.

Portrait: see *Oxford Economic Papers* (above).

HENRY HIGGS, 1864–1940

Attempts to trace the Higgs papers have not met with any success.

Correspondents

SIR HENRY CAMPBELL-BANNERMAN, correspondence with various enclosures, 1906–1919.
B.M. Add. MSS. 41240–41242.

EDWIN CANNAN, 12 letters, 1896–1933.
Cannan collection, L.S.E.

ARTHUR H. COLE, nine letters, 1929–1938.
Baker Library Archives, Harvard University.

HERBERT SOMERTON FOXWELL, copies of letters, 1890.
Collet papers.[8]

HERBERT SOMERTON FOXWELL, 12 letters, 1899.
Foxwell papers, Baker Library, Harvard University.

SIR ROBERT GIFFEN, two letters, 1895.
Giffen collection, L.S.E.

GEORGE HOWELL, two letters, 1906.
Howell papers, Bishopsgate Institute, London.

JOHN MAYNARD KEYNES, Baron Keynes, 12 letters, 1930–1936.
Keynes papers, Marshall Library, Cambridge.

JOHN NEVILLE KEYNES, two letters, 1908.
J. N. Keynes correspondence, Marshall Library, Cambridge.

MACMILLANS, several letters, 1896–1937.
B.M. Add. MS. 55198.

WILLIAM ROBERT SCOTT, two letters, 1935–1936.
Scott papers, Glasgow U.L.

WILLIAM ROBERT SCOTT, three letters, 1938.
Baker Library Archives, Harvard University.

EDWIN ROBERT ANDERSON SELIGMAN, 28 letters, 1895–1910.
Seligman papers, Columbia U.L., New York.

Printed Material

JOHN MAYNARD KEYNES, 'Henry Higgs', in *Essays in Biography*, vol. X of *Collected Writings* (London, 1972).

FRANCIS WRIGLEY HIRST, 1873–1953

From his early days in public life Hirst appears to have accumulated a considerable personal archive, which is said to have reflected his wide range of interests. The bulk of this collection, however, was destroyed or dispersed as a result of successive moves during and after the Second World War, and more of his papers may have been lost after his death in 1953. What survived was eventually placed by his widow in the custody of Mr A. F. Thompson of Wadham College, Oxford.

The remaining material consists largely of drafts for books and articles, a mass of press cuttings, and a miscellaneous collection of correspondence, most of which has no bearing on his career as an economist and economic historian. This material is not yet available for examination, but Mr Thompson is empowered to deal with enquiries.

Some lectures and notes by Hirst on Viscount Morley, with five letters to Hirst, 1928–1930.
Morley papers, India Office Library.

Correspondents

JAMES TRUSLOW ADAMS, 42 letters, 1930–1948.
Adams papers, Columbia U.L., New York.

WILLIAM HENRY BEVERIDGE, Baron Beveridge, a few letters, 1925–1933.
Beveridge papers, L.S.E.

SIR JOHN BRUNNER, 29 letters, 1909–1917.
Brunner papers, Liverpool U.L.

JOHN STEWART BRYAN, *c.* 175 items, 1924–1943.
Virginia State Library, Richmond.

SIR HENRY CAMPBELL-BANNERMAN, three letters, 1905–1907.
B.M. Add. MSS. 41238–41240.

EDWIN CANNAN, ten letters, 1915–1932.
Cannan collection, L.S.E.

JOHN BATES CLARK, two letters, 1911–1926.
Clark papers, Columbia U.L., New York.

LEONARD COURTNEY, 1st Baron Courtney of Penwith, four letters, 1915–1918.
Courtney collection, L.S.E.

SIR ROBERT ENSOR, seven letters, 1899–1904.
Ensor papers, Corpus Christi College, Oxford.

WILLIAM EWART GLADSTONE, three letters, 1895–1897.
B.M. Add. MSS. 44520–44523.

JOHN MAYNARD KEYNES, Baron Keynes, 11 letters, 1909–1920.
Keynes papers, Marshall Library, Cambridge.

OSWALD GARRISON VILLARD, 80 items, 1921–1949.
Houghton Library, Harvard University.

Printed Material
F. W. Hirst: By His Friends (London, 1958).

DNB 1951–1960, 481.

Portrait: see *F. W. Hirst: By His Friends* (above).

JOHN ATKINSON HOBSON, 1858–1940

A few letters to Hobson, including one from Herbert Spencer, with a collection of press cuttings, typescripts of papers given to the South Place Ethical Society, and his copies of his published works.
Hobson papers, Hull U.L.

Notes on a League of Nations, 1915.
Bodleian, MS. Eng. Hist. c402.

Correspondents
WILLIAM HARBUTT DAWSON, two letters, 1896–1904.
Dawson papers, Birmingham U.L.

JOHN LAWRENCE LE BRETON HAMMOND, three letters, 1907–[1930].
Bodleian, MSS. Hammond.

JOHN MAYNARD KEYNES, Baron Keynes, 13 items, 1926–1935.
Keynes papers, Marshall Library, Cambridge.

HENRY DEMAREST LLOYD, six letters, 1895–1906.
Lloyd papers, State Historical Society of Wisconsin, Madison.

MACMILLANS, several letters, 1914–1936.
B.M. Add. MS. 55209.

GILBERT MURRAY, 17 letters, 1900–1918.
Murray papers, Bodleian.

HERBERT LOUIS SAMUEL, 1st Viscount Samuel, two items, 1903.
Samuel papers, House of Lords R.O.

CHARLES PRESTWICH SCOTT, six letters, 1899.
C. P. Scott correspondence, *Manchester Guardian* Archives, Manchester J.R.U.L.

EDWIN ROBERT ANDERSON SELIGMAN, three letters, n.d.
Seligman papers, Columbia U.L., New York.

GRAHAM WALLAS, three letters, 1909–1926.
Wallas papers, L.S.E.

Printed Material

HENRY N. BRAILSFORD, *The Life-Work of J. A. Hobson* (1948).

JOHN ATKINSON HOBSON, *Confessions of an Economic Heretic* (London, 1938).

DNB 1931–1940, 435; *IESS* VI 489.

THOMAS HODGSKIN, 1787–1869

Four letters from Joseph Hume to Hodgskin, 1824–1846.
N.L.S., MS. 3112.

Three letters from Herbert Spencer to Hodgskin, 1849–1855.
Seymour collection, Knox College, Galesburg, Illinois.

A letter from James Mill to Hodgskin, 1829.
Hollander collection, University of Illinois Library, Urbana.

Correspondents

HENRY PETER BROUGHAM, 1st Baron Brougham and Vaux, six letters, 1826–1859.
Brougham papers, U.C.L.

RICHARD COBDEN, one letter (and several from Cobden to Hodgskin, 1853–1857), 1857.
Cobden papers, West Sussex R.O.

GEORGE HOWELL, one letter, 1867.
Howell papers, Bishopsgate Institute, London.

FRANCIS PLACE, 24 letters and a note on population, 1818–1822.
B.M. Add. MS. 35153.

SOCIETY FOR THE DIFFUSION OF USEFUL KNOWLEDGE, 11 letters, 1827–1828.
S.D.U.K. papers, U.C.L.

UNIVERSITY COLLEGE, LONDON, ten letters, 1834.
College correspondence, U.C.L.

Printed Material

ÉLIE HALÉVY, *Thomas Hodgskin, 1787–1869*, ed. A. J. Taylor (London, 1956).

Palgrave II 316; Boase V 676; *ESS* VII 397.

FRANCIS HORNER, 1778–1817

Correspondence, including the originals of many out-letters, 1795–1817.
Horner collection, L.S.E.

Some letters to and from Horner on the business of the Academy of Physics, Edinburgh, 1798–1799.
N.L.S., MS. 756.

Some letters, speeches, a diary Oct–Dec 1816, ten vols. of notes (some being on political economy), 1794–1804, and other papers including some on his last illness and death.
Kinnordy MSS.[18]

Correspondents

JOHN ALLEN, 32 letters, 1805–1816.
B.M. Add. MS. 52180.

JEREMY BENTHAM, five letters, 1807–1809.
B.M. Add. MS. 33544.

HENRY PETER BROUGHAM, 1st Baron Brougham and Vaux, three letters, 1811–1814.
Brougham papers, U.C.L.

ARCHIBALD CONSTABLE, six letters, 1803–1816.
N.L.S., MS. 7200.

ELIZABETH FOX, Lady Holland, four letters (and many of her letters to him), 1811–1817.
B.M. Add. MS. 51644.

CHARLES GREY, 2nd Earl Grey, ten letters, 1809–1817.
Grey of Howick papers, Durham D.P.

SIR JAMES MACKINTOSH, one letter and enclosure, 1813.
B.M. Add. MS. 52452.

JAMES REDDIE, many letters, 1803–1815.
N.L.S., MS. 3704.

RICHARD SHARP, a letter and a draft of the Bullion Resolutions, 1811.
Kress Library, Harvard University.

SAMUEL WHITBREAD, five letters, 1808–1811.
Whitbread papers, Bedfordshire R.O.

Printed Material

LEONARD HORNER, *Memoirs and Correspondence of Francis Horner, M.P.*, 2 vols. (London, 1843).
The second (American) edition, 1853, contains more letters than the first edition.

The Economic Writings of Francis Horner in the Edinburgh Review, 1802–6, ed. Frank Whitson Fetter (London, 1957).

Palgrave II 331; *DNB* IX 1265.

Portraits: B.M.(P); N.P.G.; S.N.G.; S.N.P.G.

DAVID HUME, 1711–1776

Correspondence, consisting of 525 letters to Hume, some from economists, and 159 letters of Hume, including those to Adam Smith and Francis Hutcheson. Also a small group of letters about Hume from just before and after his death, 1775–1776. Some manuscripts of verses, notes, memoranda and his published works, plus papers not in Hume's hand. 13 bound volumes in all.
Hume papers, Royal Society of Edinburgh.

Notes and corrected proofs for some of his published works.
N.L.S., MSS. 509, 732–734, 786, 1703.

His manuscript account, with copies of correspondence, of the quarrel with Rousseau.
N.L.S., MS. 5722.

A memorandum on Canadian paper money, with two related letters of 1765.
N.L.S., MS. 2619.

His diary of the 1746 military expedition to Port L'Orient.
B.M. Add. MS. 36638.

Printed Material

The Letters of David Hume, ed. John Young Thomson Greig, 2 vols. (Oxford, 1932).
The first volume has letters, 1727–1765, and the second 1766–1776.

New Letters of David Hume, ed. E. C. Mossner and R. Klibansky (Oxford, 1954).
Includes the letters which have been discovered since Greig's volumes appeared.

DAVID HUME, *Writings on Economics*, ed. E. Rotwein (London, 1955).
A collection of Hume's writings from various sources which deal with economic questions.

Palgrave II 340; *DNB* X 215; *ESS* VII 550; *IESS* VI 546.

Portraits: B.M. (P); N.P.G.; S.N.P.G.; Edinburgh University.

JAMES DEACON HUME, 1774–1842

His political and administrative papers passed to his successor at the Board of Trade, John MacGregor, and have since been lost. The letter books of the Board of Trade contain many copies of letters sent by Hume on the business of the Board.
Board of Trade papers, P.R.O.

Correspondents

RICHARD COBDEN, one letter, 1841.
Cobden papers, West Sussex R.O.

ROYAL SOCIETY OF ARTS, four letters, 1796–1797.
Royal Society of Arts Library, London.

GEORGE JOHN SPENCER, 2nd Earl Spencer, five letters, 1805–1816.
Spencer papers, N.R.A. 10410.

AUGUSTUS GRANVILLE STAPLETON, seven items, *c.* 1830.
London U.L., MS. 636.

Printed Material

CHARLES BADHAM, *The Life of James Deacon Hume* (London, 1859).

Palgrave II 343; *DNB* X 228.

JOSEPH HUME, 1777–1855

A group of letters to various correspondents, 1822–1852.
N.L.S., MS. 3397.

Nine letters to various correspondents, 1822–1852.
Aberdeen U.L., MSS. 2135, 2271.

A few letters to and from various correspondents, on behalf of Jeremy Bentham, 1816–1830.
Bentham MSS., U.C.L.

Seven letters to various correspondents, 1813–1834.
Foxwell collection, Baker Library, Harvard University.

Correspondents

EDWARD BAINES, two letters, 1836–1848.
Baines papers, Leeds City Library, Archives Dept.

JEREMY BENTHAM, five letters, 1829–1830.
B.M. Add. MS. 33546.

HENRY PETER BROUGHAM, 1st Baron Brougham and Vaux, 54 letters, 1826–1853.
Brougham papers, U.C.L.

JOHN HILL BURTON, 20 letters, 1838–1854.
N.L.S., MS. 9404.

GEORGE CANNING, several letters, 1822–1826.
Canning papers, Leeds City Library, Archives Dept.

EDWIN CHADWICK, 42 letters, 1831–1849.
Chadwick papers, U.C.L.

THOMAS CHALMERS, two letters, 1832.
Chalmers papers, New College, Edinburgh.

RICHARD COBDEN, *c.* 200 items, 1839–1854.
B.M. Add. MS. 43668.

F. A. COX, five letters, 1825–1828.
Marischal College Archives, Aberdeen U.L.

EDWARD DAVIES DAVENPORT, seven letters, 1835–1846.
Bromley-Davenport Muniments, Manchester J.R.U.L.

BENJAMIN DISRAELI, Earl of Beaconsfield, 12 letters, 1850–1852.
Disraeli papers, N.R.A. 0842.

WILLIAM EWART GLADSTONE, 11 letters, 1846–1854.
B.M. Add. MSS: 44363–44584.

GEORGE HAMILTON GORDON, 4th Earl of Aberdeen, *c.* 90 items, 1829–1854.
B.M. Add. MS. 43200.

HENRY GEORGE GREY, 3rd Earl Grey, 15 letters, 1831–1849.
Grey of Howick papers, Durham D.P.

JOHN CHARLES HERRIES, several letters, 1852–1853.
B.M. Add. MSS. 57366–57469.

THOMAS HODGSKIN, four letters, 1824–1846.
N.L.S., MS. 3112.

GEORGE JACOB HOLYOAKE, three letters, 1844.
Holyoake collection, Co-operative Union Ltd, Manchester.

WILLIAM HUSKISSON, four items, 1825.
B.M. Add. MS. 38747.

ROBERT BANKS JENKINSON, 2nd Earl of Liverpool, five items, 1813–1823.
B.M. Add. MSS. 38292–38410.

JOHN LEE, six letters, 1831–1838.
N.L.S., Lee papers.

PETER MACKENZIE, *c.* 20 letters, 1831–1858.
Mackenzie papers, N.R.A. 11630.

HORACE MANN, eight letters, n.d.
Horace Mann papers, Library of the Massachusetts Historical Society, Boston.

SIR WILLIAM NAPIER, several letters, 1833–1851.
Bodleian, MS. Eng. Lett. c251.

ROBERT OWEN, three letters, 1830–1832.
Robert Owen correspondence, Co-operative Union Ltd, Manchester.

R. PAGE, 12 letters, 1839–1841.
Bodleian, MS. Eng. Lett. b3.

SIR ROBERT PEEL, *c.* 70 items, 1822–1848.
B.M. Add. MSS. 40344–40600.

FRANCIS PLACE, many letters, 1814–1841.
B.M. Add. MSS. 35145–35151, 37949–37950.

ADOLPHE QUÉTELET, four letters, 1833–1845.
Quételet papers, Bibliothèque Royale de Belgique, Brussels.

SIR JOHN and SIR GEORGE SINCLAIR, *c.* 60 letters, 1812–1853.
Sinclair of Ulbster papers, N.R.A. 10552.

JOHN BENJAMIN SMITH, nine letters, 1840–1841.
J. B. Smith papers, Manchester City Library.

HENRY JOHN TEMPLE, 3rd Viscount Palmerston, eight letters, 1836–1851.
Broadlands papers, N.R.A. 12889.

SAMUEL WHITBREAD, four letters, 1813–1814.
Whitbread papers, Bedfordshire R.O.

SIR ROBERT JOHN WILMOT-HORTON, four letters, 1823–1826.
Catton collection, Derby Borough Library.

GEORGE WILSON, five letters, 1839–1850.
Wilson papers, Manchester City Library.

Printed Material
Palgrave II 343; *DNB* x 230; Boase I 1586.

Portraits: B.M.(P); N.P.G.; U.C.L.; House of Commons Library.

WILLIAM HUSKISSON, 1770–1830

Correspondence, official and private, 1782–1830, with other papers, including notes and drafts for speeches.
B.M. Add. MSS. 38734–38770, 39948–39949.

Correspondence received through the Liverpool Parliamentary Office and many copies of out-letters, 1814–1830.
Liverpool Parliamentary Office papers, Liverpool R.O.

A group of papers used in the negotiations over the Canadian–U.S. boundary, 1824–1826.
Western Americana collection, Yale U.L.

Correspondents
WILLIAM DACRES ADAMS, ten letters, 1801–1809.
Adams papers, P.R.O.

GEORGE CANNING, several letters, 1789–1822.
Canning papers, Leeds City Library, Archives Dept.

JOHN EVELYN DENISON, five letters, 1828–1830.
Denison papers, Nottingham U.L.

HENRY DUNDAS, 1st Viscount Melville, nine letters, 1797–1800.
Melville Castle Muniments, Scottish R.O.

HENRY DUNDAS, 1st Viscount Melville, 14 letters, 1794–1810 (with other assorted correspondence).
Melville papers, W. L. Clements Library, University of Michigan, Ann Arbor.

ROBERT DUNDAS, 2nd Viscount Melville, eight letters, 1808–1824.
Melville papers, W. L. Clements Library, University of Michigan, Ann Arbor.

JOHN FOSTER, 1st Baron Oriel, 14 letters, 1807–1809.
Foster/Massereene papers, P.R.O.N.I.

SIR JAMES WILLOUGHBY GORDON, 50 letters, 1805–1821.
B.M. Add. MS. 49479.

ROBERT BANKS JENKINSON, 2nd Earl of Liverpool, many letters, 1806–1826.
B.M. Add. MS. 38191.

GRANVILLE LEVESON-GOWER, 1st Earl Granville, 46 letters, 1799–1830.
Granville papers, P.R.O.

JOHN PARKER, 1st Earl of Morley, several letters, 1827.
B.M. Add. MSS. 48218–48301.

SIR ROBERT PEEL, *c.* 300 items, 1822–1828.
B.M. Add. MSS. 40333–40397.

WILLIAM PITT the Younger, 16 letters, n.d.
Chatham papers, P.R.O.

GEORGE RAMSAY, 9th Earl of Dalhousie, several items, 1827–1828.
Dalhousie papers, Scottish R.O.

DAVID SCOTT, 15 letters, 1796–1824.
Birmingham U.L., Add. Letters 1114–1130.

SIR ROBERT JOHN WILMOT-HORTON, ten letters, 1806–1830.
Catton collection, Derby Borough Library.

Printed Material

CHARLES RYLE FAY, *Huskisson and his Age* (London, 1951).

LEWIS MELVILLE, *The Huskisson Papers* (London, 1931).

Palgrave II 345; *DNB* X 323; *ESS* VII 559.

Portraits: N.P.G.; Courtauld Institute; statue in Pimlico Gardens.

JOHN KELLS INGRAM, 1823–1907

Correspondence, 1850–1906, with family, economists, positivists and others. Also many miscellaneous papers, printed books, photographs.
Ingram papers, P.R.O.N.I.

Some papers from his work for the Royal Irish Academy and the Brehon Law Commissioners. Notebooks and lectures on literary topics.
Trinity College, Dublin.

Correspondents

RICHARD CONGREVE, six letters (and *c.* 150 of Congreve's to Ingram), 1861–1899.
B.M. Add. MSS. 45228, 45233.

RICHARD THEODORE ELY, four letters, 1880s.
Ely papers, University of Wisconsin, Madison.

WILLIAM EWART GLADSTONE, nine letters, 1873.
B.M. Add. MSS. 44437–44438.

WILLIAM STANLEY JEVONS, two letters, 1881.
Jevons papers, Manchester J.R.U.L.

THOMAS EDWARD CLIFFE LESLIE, one letter, 1878.
London U.L., A.L. 63.

Printed Material

C. L. FALKINER, *Memoir of John Kells Ingram* (Dublin, 1907).

Bibliography of the Writings of John Kells Ingram, 1823–1907 (Dublin, 1909).

ESS VIII 34.

Portrait: see *Centenary History of the Statistical and Social Inquiry Society of Ireland* ed. R. D. Collison Black (Dublin, 1947).

HENRY CHARLES FLEEMING JENKIN, 1833–1885

A few letters to Jenkin (three from James Clerk Maxwell, 1874–1876, two from George Burnett, 1883, three from Alfred Austin, 1875–1883, and four from Clementine Sterling Graham, 1875). Other family letters, etc., which concern Jenkin.
Jenkin papers, N.R.A. 16603.

15 letters and reports on papers.
Royal Society Library, London.

Correspondents
WILLIAM STANLEY JEVONS, three letters, 1868.
Jevons papers, Manchester J.R.U.L.

JAMES CLERK MAXWELL four letters, n.d.
Cambridge U.L., MS. 7655.

JAMES THOMSON, five letters, 1874–1882.
Thompson papers, Queen's University, Belfast.

WILLIAM THOMSON, Baron Kelvin, several letters, n.d.
Kelvin papers, Dept. of Natural Philosophy, Glasgow University.

Printed Material
H. C. F. JENKIN, *Papers Literary and Scientific*, 2 vols. (London, 1887).
Contains a memoir of Jenkin by Robert Louis Stevenson.

Palgrave II 473; *DNB* X 733; Boase II 76; *ESS* VIII 380.

Portrait: see *Papers Literary and Scientific* (above).

WILLIAM STANLEY JEVONS, 1835–1882

Personal and professional papers, the former consisting of correspondence with other members of the Jevons family and his journals, the latter of his correspondence with economists, the manuscripts of his published books and articles, and

other related papers. The papers are not available for examination until after completion of the publication of the *Papers and Correspondence*, noted below.
Jevons papers, Manchester J.R.U.L.

Tables of statistics, charts and some other manuscripts mainly connected with the circulation of gold coins.
Royal Statistical Society.[19]

Notes taken by Jevons from the mathematical lectures of Augustus de Morgan, 1852–1853 and 1860–1861, and also from de Morgan's published mathematical tracts.
Glasgow U.L.

Printed Material

Papers and Correspondence of William Stanley Jevons, ed. R. D. Collison Black, 4 vols., in progress (London, 1972–).

Vol. III, when it appears, will consist of Jevons's correspondence, 1863–1882, which is largely of a professional nature.

Palgrave II 474; *DNB* X 811; Boase II 96; *ESS* VIII 389; *IESS* VIII 254.

Portraits: N.P.G. (A); see *Papers and Correspondence* (above).

RICHARD JONES, 1790–1855

Jones's papers, from which his *Literary Remains* were edited, were owned by his widow. Her descendants do not have the papers.

His letters from William Whewell, 285 in number, 1817–1854, which were returned to Whewell. Also a box of letters and notes arising from Whewell's editorship of the *Literary Remains*.
Whewell papers, Trinity College, Cambridge.

A memorandum of observations on Mr Buller's proposals on the Tithe Bill, 1836, in a secretary's hand.
Grey of Howick papers, Durham D.P.

Correspondents

CHARLES BABBAGE, six letters, 1832–1838.
B.M. Add. MSS. 37186–37191.

HENRY PETER BROUGHAM, 1st Baron Brougham and Vaux, two letters, 1853.
Brougham papers, U.C.L.

SIR JOHN FREDERICK WILLIAM HERSCHEL, 75 items, 1816–1853.
Herschel papers, Royal Society Library, London.

SIR ROBERT PEEL, four items, 1841–1844.
B.M. Add. MSS. 40488–40546.

WILLIAM WHEWELL, 184 letters, 1821–1854.
Whewell papers, Trinity College, Cambridge.

Printed Material

L. G. JOHNSON, *Richard Jones Reconsidered* (1955).

RICHARD JONES, *Literary Remains*, ed. William Whewell (Hertford, 1859).

Palgrave II 490; *DNB* X 1045; Boase II 140; *ESS* VIII 415.

Portrait: B.M. (P).

THOMAS JOPLIN, 1790–1847

Joplin died in poverty in Silesia, and his papers are not known to exist.

Correspondents

HENRY PETER BROUGHAM, 1st Baron Brougham and Vaux, two letters, 1843–1844.
Brougham papers, U.C.L.

JOSEPH HUME, five letters, 1824–1832.
London U.L., A.L.s. 64, 66, 67.

WILLIAM JORDAN, one letter, 1824.
Bodleian, MS. Eng. Lett. d113.

SIR EDWARD KNATCHBULL, two letters, 1831–1844.
London U.L., A.L.s 65, 68.

SIR ROBERT PEEL, four items, 1823–1841.
B.M. Add. MSS. 40354–40495.

Printed Material
DNB x 1079.

JOHN MAYNARD KEYNES, BARON KEYNES, 1883–1946

Professional papers, in subject groupings each with relevant correspondence, including material on official work, manuscripts of books, articles, lectures, broadcasts, etc.; papers from his work for various societies, business organisations and educational establishments.
Keynes papers, Marshall Library, Cambridge.

Personal papers, comprising family correspondence, 1897–1946; material on book and picture collecting, theatre and ballet (with some papers of Lydia Lopokova); King's College business, all with related correspondence.
Keynes papers, King's College, Cambridge.

Printed Material
R. F. HARROD, *The Life of John Maynard Keynes* (London, 1951).

The Collected Works of John Maynard Keynes, ed. Elizabeth Johnson and Donald Moggeridge (London, 1971–).
This 25-volume edition of Keynes's works and papers includes Keynes's correspondence.

DNB 1941–1950, 452; *IESS* VIII 368.

Portraits: N.P.G.; see Harrod and *Collected Works* (above).

JOHN NEVILLE KEYNES, 1852–1949

Diaries, 1864–1917, with a few gaps, in 40 volumes. They deal with academic and family affairs, including accounts of his reading, the progress of his books, meetings of societies and committees, conversations and correspondence.
Cambridge U.L., Add. MSS. 7827–7867.

About 250 letters to Keynes, 1872–1918, on family and university matters, with a few from economists.
Cambridge U.L., Add. MS. 7562.

About 400 letters to him, 1891–1942 (but mainly pre-1900).
Marshall Library, Cambridge.

Notebooks, four with material probably collected for a new edition of his *Formal Logic*, post-1884, and six containing notes on his reading, mainly on economics, *c.* 1875.
Pembroke College, Cambridge.

Seven volumes of notes, mainly from Henry Sidgwick's lectures on philosophy and ethics, 1874–1876.
King's College, Cambridge.

Two volumes of collected examination questions on logic, mainly from the 1870s and 1880s.
Cambridge U.L., Add. MSS. 7322–7323.

Correspondents

HERBERT SOMERTON FOXWELL, five letters, 1902–1916.
Marshall Library, Cambridge.

HERBERT SOMERTON FOXWELL, five letters, 1900.
Foxwell papers, Baker Library, Harvard University.

CHRISTINE LADD FRANKLIN, three letters, 1903–1905.
Franklin papers, Columbia U.L., New York.

FRANCIS JOHN HENRY JENKINSON, ten letters, 1893–1919.
Cambridge U.L., Add. MS. 6463.

MACMILLANS, many letters, 1883–1941.
B.M. Add. MS. 55207.

ALFRED MARSHALL, four letters, 1884–1902.
Marshall papers, Marshall Library, Cambridge.

SIR ROBERT HARRY INGLIS PALGRAVE, three letters, 1886–1887.
Palgrave papers.[9]

Printed Material

IESS VIII 376.

Portrait: N.P.G.(A).

THOMAS EDWARD CLIFFE LESLIE, 1825–1882

Letters and testimonials connected with his academic appointments, 1873–1882.
Registered papers, State Paper Office (Dublin Castle).

Correspondents

JOHN ELLIOT CAIRNES, eight items, 1862–1863.
N.L.I., MS. 8955.

EDWIN CHADWICK, three letters, n.d.
Chadwick papers, U.C.L.

WILLIAM EWART GLADSTONE, two letters, 1867–1873.
B.M. Add. MSS. 44413–44437.

JOHN KELLS INGRAM, *c.* 60 letters, mainly n.d.
Ingram papers, P.R.O.N.I.

WILLIAM STANLEY JEVONS, two letters, 1878–1879.
Jevons papers, Manchester J.R.U.L.

JOHN STUART MILL, two letters, 1870.
Mill–Taylor collection, L.S.E.

JOHN STUART MILL, letter or letters, n.d.
Mill papers, Yale U.L.

CHARLES HENRY PEARSON, two letters, 1879.
Bodleian, MS. Eng. Lett. d189.

HELEN TAYLOR, a few letters, 1867–1878?
Mill–Taylor collection, L.S.E.

LÉON WALRAS, three letters, 1874–1879.
Fonds Walras, Bibliothèque Cantonale et Universitaire, Lausanne.

Printed Material

Palgrave II 596; *DNB* XI 987; Boase II 397; *ESS* IX 417; *IESS* IX 260.

LEONE LEVI, 1821–1888

The manuscripts of his *Commercial Law, its Principles and Administration* and *Commentaries on Commercial Law*.
Biblioteca Civica, Ancona, Italy.

Correspondents

HENRY PETER BROUGHAM, 1st Baron Brougham and Vaux, 36 letters, 1850–1864.
Brougham papers, U.C.L.

RICHARD COBDEN, and MRS COBDEN, three letters, 1862–1867.
Cobden papers, West Sussex R.O.

BENJAMIN DISRAELI, Earl of Beaconsfield, two letters, 1849–1863.
Disraeli papers, N.R.A. 0842.

WILLIAM EWART GLADSTONE, five letters, 1860–1867.
B.M. Add. MSS. 44393–44452.

GEORGE HOWELL, three letters, 1874–1875.
Howell papers, Bishopsgate Institute, London.

HENRY RICHARD, two letters, 1878–1887.
N.L.W., MS. 5505.

GEORGE WILSON, two letters, 1865–1870.
Wilson papers, Manchester City Library.

Printed Material

LEONI LEVI, *The Story of My Life* (London, 1888).

Palgrave II 598; *DNB* XI 1035; Boase II 405; *ESS* IX 424.

Portrait: N.P.G. (A).

ROBERT LOWE, 1st VISCOUNT SHERBROOKE, 1811–1892

Some family papers, *c.* 1820–1892, including letters to and from Lowe, and a few from politicians.
Lowe papers, N.R.A. 8681.

Correspondents

HENRY PETER BROUGHAM, 1st Baron Brougham and Vaux, four letters, 1862–1864.
Brougham papers, U.C.L.

EDWARD CARDWELL, official correspondence, 1868–1874.
Cardwell papers, P.R.O.

WILLIAM EWART GLADSTONE, many letters, 1852–1885.
B.M. Add. MSS. 44301–44302.

WILLIAM STANLEY JEVONS, two letters, 1871–1878.
Jevons papers, Manchester J.R.U.L.

EDWARD HUGESSEN KNATCHBULL-HUGESSEN, 1st Baron Brabourne, three letters, 1857–1869.
Knatchbull papers, Kent Archives Office.

GRANVILLE GEORGE LEVESON-GOWER, 2nd Earl Granville, one volume of correspondence, 1869–1873.
Granville papers, P.R.O.

SAMUEL JONES LOYD, Baron Overstone, two letters, 1858–1861.
Overstone papers, London U.L., MS. 804.

ROUNDELL PALMER, 1st Earl of Selborne, three items, 1872.
Selborne papers, Lambeth Palace Library, London.

LYON PLAYFAIR, 1st Baron Playfair of St Andrews, five letters, 1868–1879.
Playfair papers, Imperial College Archives, London.

GEORGE FREDERICK SAMUEL ROBINSON, 2nd Earl of Ripon, 18 letters, 1869–1873.
B.M. Add. MS. 43532.

JAMES EDWIN THOROLD ROGERS, two letters, 1875–1878.
Thorold Rogers papers, N.R.A. 12396.

A. C. TUPP, several letters, 1874–1881.
Bodleian, MS. Eng. Lett. d148.

GEORGE WILLIAM FREDERICK VILLIERS, 4th Earl of Clarendon, several letters, 1868–1870.
Bodleian, MS. Clar. Dep. c499.

Printed Material

J. F. HOGAN, *Robert Lowe, Viscount Sherbrooke* (London, 1893).

ARTHUR PATCHETT MARTIN, *Life and Letters of the Right Honourable Robert Lowe, Viscount Sherbrooke*, 2 vols. (London, 1893).

Palgrave III 391; *DNB* VII 197.

Portrait: see Ruth A. Knight, *Illiberal Liberal: Robert Lowe in New South Wales, 1842–1850* (Carlton, Australia, 1966).

SAMUEL JONES LOYD, BARON OVERSTONE, 1796–1883

Correspondence, 1804–1883, with other papers on economics, politics and family matters.
Overstone papers, London U.L., MS. 804.

Correspondents

CHARLES BABBAGE, six letters, 1834–1849.
B.M. Add. MSS. 37188–37194.

JOHN ELLIOT CAIRNES, two letters, 1857–1859.
N.L.I., MS. 8944.

EDWARD CARDWELL, copies of correspondence, 1858.
B.M. Add. MS. 44118.

EDWIN CHADWICK, four letters, 1836–1839.
Chadwick papers, U.C.L.

BENJAMIN DISRAELI, Earl of Beaconsfield, two letters, 1859.
Disraeli papers, N.R.A. 0842.

WILLIAM EWART GLADSTONE, six letters, 1853–1865.
B.M. Add. MSS. 44373–44406.

HENRY GEORGE GREY, 3rd Earl Grey, two letters, 1872–1881.
Grey of Howick papers, Durham D.P.

GRANVILLE GEORGE LEVESON-GOWER, 2nd Earl Granville, nine letters, 1853–1872.
Granville papers, P.R.O.

SIR GEORGE CORNEWALL LEWIS, five letters, 1856–1857.
Harpton Court papers, N.L.W.

SIR JOHN WILLIAM LUBBOCK, three letters, 1851–1855.
Lubbock papers, Royal Society Library, London.

LORD JOHN RUSSELL, 1st Earl Russell, two letters, 1846–1849.
Russell papers, P.R.O.

JOHN BENJAMIN SMITH, four items, 1840.
J. B. Smith papers, Manchester City Library.

GEORGE JOHN SPENCER, 2nd Earl Spencer, some letters, n.d.
Spencer papers, N.R.A. 10410.

THOMAS SPRING-RICE, 1st Baron Monteagle, some letters, n.d.
Monteagle papers, N.L.I.

SAMUEL WILBERFORCE, five letters, 1850–1864.
Bodleian, MSS. Wilberforce.

CHARLES WOOD, 1st Viscount Halifax, about ten letters, 1846–1881.
Hickleton papers, N.R.A. 8128.

Printed Material

The Correspondence of Lord Overstone, ed. Denis Patrick O'Brien, 3 vols. (London, 1972).

Palgrave II 647; *DNB* XII 224; Boase II 1281; *ESS* XI 517.

Portrait: see *Correspondence* (above).

JOHN RAMSEY McCULLOCH, 1789–1864

Professor Denis O'Brien reports that on contacting a descendant of McCulloch, he was informed that his papers had comparatively recently been destroyed.

41 letters from David Ricardo, 1816–1823.
B.M. Add. MS. 34545.

39 letters from various correspondents, 1820–1863.
London U.L., A.L.s 57, 187, 271, 413.

About 25 letters connected with his Chair of Political Economy at University College, London.
College correspondence, U.C.L.

Four letters to various correspondents, 1823–1838.
Hollander collection, University of Illinois Library, Urbana.

Records of his work at His Majesty's Stationery Office.
Stationery Office Records and Comptroller's Private Letter-book, P.R.O.

A note on gold currency in India.
Halifax papers, India Office Library.

Correspondents

EDWARD GEORGE EARLE LYTTON BULWER-LYTTON, Baron Lytton, two letters, 1851.
Bulwer-Lytton papers, Hertfordshire R.O.

EDWIN CHADWICK, three items, 1841–1852.
Chadwick papers, U.C.L.

BENJAMIN DISRAELI, Earl of Beaconsfield, 24 letters, 1848–1863.
Disraeli papers, N.R.A. 0842.

WILLIAM EWART GLADSTONE, five letters, 1853–1859.
B.M. Add. MSS. 44381–44392.

HENRY GEORGE GREY, 3rd Earl Grey, three letters, 1844–1856.
Grey of Howick papers, Durham D.P.

WILLIAM HUSKISSON, a few letters, 1825.
B.M. Add. MS. 38746.

SIR GEORGE CORNEWALL LEWIS, ten letters, 1846–1863.
Harpton Court papers, N.L.W.

SAMUEL JONES LOYD, Baron Overstone, 20 letters, 1856–1864.
Overstone papers, London U.L., MS. 804.

JOHN MURRAY, several letters, n.d.
Archives of John Murray Ltd.[17]

MACVEY NAPIER, 70 letters, 1817–1847.
B.M. Add. MSS. 34612–34630.

SIR ROBERT PEEL, *c.* 25 items, 1842–1850.
B.M. Add. MSS. 40512–40603.

FRANCIS PLACE, four letters, 1820–1827.
B.M. Add. MS. 37949.

DAVID RICARDO, 35 letters, 1816–1823.
Ricardo papers, Cambridge U.L., Add. MS. 7510.

WILLIAM RITCHIE, about ten letters (with related accounts and other material), 1820–1824 and n.d.
William Ritchie's MSS.[10]

SOCIETY FOR THE DIFFUSION OF USEFUL KNOWLEDGE, many letters, n.d.
S.D.U.K. papers, U.C.L.

THOMAS SPRING-RICE, 1st Baron Monteagle, some letters, n.d.
Monteagle papers, N.L.I.

JOHN STRANG, ten letters, 1852–1860.
Records of the Dilettante Society of Glasgow, Glasgow City Archives.

SIR ROBERT JOHN WILMOT-HORTON, 16 letters, 1826–1831.
Catton collection, Derby Borough Library.

Printed Material
DENIS PATRICK O'BRIEN, *J. R. McCulloch* (London, 1970).

Palgrave II 657; *DNB* XII 463; Boase II 579; *ESS* IX 649; *IESS* IX 501.

Portrait: N.P.G.

HENRY DUNNING MACLEOD, 1821–1902

Published works, and printed documents concerning his petition of right to the Crown for compensation for work done on a digest of the laws of bills of exchange. Also ten letters, 1898–1900, to his son, R. H. Macleod, on a gold standard for India.
Macleod papers.[11]

A group of seven letters, 1870–1871, to various correspondents.
Edinburgh U.L.

Correspondents
JOHN HILL BURTON, nine letters, 1860–1871.
N.L.S., MS. 9396 *et seq.*

EDWIN CHADWICK, ten items, 1859–1889.
Chadwick papers, U.C.L.

JOHN KELLS INGRAM, two letters, 1886–1892.
Ingram papers, P.R.O.N.I.

LÉON WALRAS, three letters, 1875–1888.
Fonds Walras, Bibliothèque Cantonale et Universitaire, Lausanne.

REGINALD EARLE WELBY, 1st Baron Welby, a letter and a memorandum, 1895–1899.
Welby collection, L.S.E.

Printed Material
DNB 1901–1911, 540; *ESS* x 30.

JAMES MAITLAND, 8th EARL OF LAUDERDALE, 1759–1839

Manuscript of *Three Letters to the Duke of Wellington on the Fourth Report of the Committee of Finance*, 1829. No other papers of the 8th Earl of Lauderdale.
Lauderdale MSS.[16]

14 letters, some from Lauderdale, 1815–1819, on the financial arrangements of Lord Deerhurst.
N.L.S., MS. 9818.

Copy of a document compiled by Lauderdale and others, 1783, in the case of T. Muir and T. Fyshe Palmer.
Whitbread papers, Bedfordshire R.O.

Correspondents
WILLIAM ADAM, many letters, 1790–1830.
Adam papers, N.R.A. 9954.

JOHN ALLEN, 14 letters, 1806–1830.
B.M. Add. MS. 52180.

HENRY PETER BROUGHAM, 1st Baron Brougham and Vaux, six letters, 1808–1827.
Brougham papers, U.C.L.

ARCHIBALD CONSTABLE, six letters, 1814–1825.
N.L.S., MSS. 789–792.

CHARLES JAMES FOX, 16 letters, 1806 (and *c.* 200 from Fox to Lauderdale, 1796–1806).
B.M. Add. MSS. 47564, 51458.

ELIZABETH FOX, Lady Holland, ten volumes of letters, 1799–1839.
B.M. Add. MSS. 51695–51704.

HENRY RICHARD VASSALL FOX, 3rd Baron Holland, four volumes of letters, 1797–1838.
B.M. Add. MSS. 51691–51694.

ROBERT HAMILTON, four letters, 1813–1818.
Hamilton papers, Aberdeen U.L.

THOMAS GRANVILLE, three letters, 1807.
B.M. Add. MS. 41857.

CHARLES GREY, 2nd Earl Grey, many letters, 1800–1839.
Grey of Howick papers, Durham D.P.

WILLIAM HUSKISSON, three items, 1815–1824.
B.M. Add. MSS. 38740–38745.

ROBERT BANKS JENKINSON, 2nd Earl of Liverpool, five letters, 1810–1818.
B.M. Add. MSS. 38254–38410.

SIR ROBERT PEEL, *c.* 20 items, 1822–1832.
B.M. Add. MSS. 40347–40402.

WILLIAM PITT the Younger, three letters, n.d.
Chatham papers, P.R.O.

JOHN SCOTT, 1st Earl of Eldon, copies of correspondence, 1809.
N.L.S., MS. 9.

GEORGE JOHN SPENCER, 2nd Earl Spencer, five letters, 1807–1824.
Spencer papers, N.R.A. 10410.

SAMUEL WHITBREAD, three letters, 1792–1808.
Whitbread papers, Bedfordshire R.O.

Printed Material
Palgrave II 574; *DNB* XII 799; *ESS* IX 191; *IESS* IX 47.
Portraits: N.P.G.; S.N.P.G.

SIR LOUIS MALLET, 1823–1890

Two large boxes of mainly official papers and correspondence, connected with his work at the Board of Trade, 1847–1872, and the India Office, 1872–1883.
Mallet papers.[6]

Papers connected with the work of the Anglo-Austrian Tariff Commission, 1867.
B.M. Add. MSS. 38814–38815.

43 letters to Mallet, 1876–1878, mainly from Lord Lytton.
Lytton papers, India Office Library.

14 items, including letters to and from various correspondents, 1878–1885.
Welby collection, L.S.E.

Correspondents

JOHN BRIGHT, five letters, 1861–1872.
B.M. Add. MS. 43389.

SIR JAMES CAIRD, four items, 1878–1879.
Home miscellaneous MSS., India Office Library.

EDWIN CHADWICK, 24 letters, 1873–1889.
Chadwick papers, U.C.L.

RICHARD COBDEN, 34 letters, 1860–1865.
B.M. Add. MS. 43666.

RICHARD COBDEN, more letters, 1860–1865.
Cobden papers, West Sussex R.O.

BENJAMIN DISRAELI, Earl of Beaconsfield, two letters, 1877.
Disraeli papers, N.R.A. 0842.

ROBERT ARTHUR TALBOT GASCOYNE-CECIL, 3rd Marquess of Salisbury, 146 letters, 1874–1888.
Salisbury papers, Christ Church College, Oxford.

GATHORNE GATHORNE-HARDY, 1st Earl of Cranbrook, several letters, 1878–1879.
Cranbrook papers, Ipswich and East Suffolk R.O.

WILLIAM EWART GLADSTONE, seven letters, 1867–1882.
B.M. Add. MSS. 44412–44477.

JOHN ARTHUR GODLEY, 1st Baron Kilbracken, five letters, 1885.
Kilbracken papers, India Office Library.

JOHN JAY, two letters, 1872–1874.
Jay papers, Columbia U.L., New York.

SIR AUSTEN HENRY LAYARD, 33 items, 1865–1866.
B.M. Add. MSS. 38992–39119.

RALPH ROBERT WHEELER LINGEN, 1st Baron Lingen, six items, 1878–1879.
Welby Collection, L.S.E.

FLORENCE NIGHTINGALE, three letters, 1875–1885.
B.M. Add. MS. 45779.

SIR ROBERT HARRY INGLIS PALGRAVE, three letters, 1873–1875.
Palgrave papers.[9]

GEORGE FREDERICK SAMUEL ROBINSON, 2nd Earl of Ripon, seven letters, 1880–1882.
B.M. Add. MSS. 43627–43632.

JAMES EDWIN THOROLD ROGERS, nine letters, 1868–1889.
Thorold Rogers papers, N.R.A. 12396.

HENRY SIDGWICK, four letters, 1886–1887.
Sidgwick papers, Trinity College, Cambridge.

GEORGE WILLIAM FREDERICK VILLIERS, 4th Earl of Clarendon, letters to and from, 1865–1870.
Bodleian, MSS. Clar. Dep. c91, c145, c499–500.

SIR PHILIP WODEHOUSE, 11 letters, n.d.
Wodehouse correspondence, India Office Library.

Printed Material

BERNARD MALLET, *Sir Louis Mallet* (London, 1905).

Palgrave II 666; *DNB* XII 872; Boase II 711.

Portrait: see Bernard Mallet (above).

THOMAS ROBERT MALTHUS, 1766–1834

Journals of his tours on the continent, 1799–1826.
Cambridge U.L., Add. MSS. 7704–7709.

Manuscript of the *Principles of Political Economy*, mainly chapters on wealth and labour, value, rent, with a few corrected proof sheets; 264 pages, 1820. Also an annotated copy of the *Principles.*
Marshall Library, Cambridge.

Letters from David Ricardo, 1811–1823, are kept with the Ricardo papers.
Cambridge U.L., Add. MS. 7510.

Correspondents

THOMAS CHALMERS seven letters, 1821–1833.
Chalmers papers, New College, Edinburgh.

ALEXANDER JOHN GASPARD MARCET, three letters, 1807–1815.
Seligman collection, Columbia U.L., New York.

JOHN MURRAY, 36 letters, 1815–1834.
Archives of John Murray Ltd.[17]

MACVEY NAPIER, 11 letters, 1814–1830.
B.M. Add. MSS. 34611–34614.

HENRY BROOKE PARNELL, 1st Baron Congleton, two letters, 1808.
Congleton papers.[12]

PIERRE PRÉVOST, six letters, 1815–1824.
Prévost MSS., Bibliothèque Publique et Universitaire de Genève.

DAVID RICARDO, 75 letters, 1811–1833.
Ricardo papers, Cambridge U.L., Add. MS. 7510.

WILLIAM WHEWELL, four letters, 1829–1833.
Whewell papers, Trinity College, Cambridge.

SIR ROBERT JOHN WILMOT-HORTON, 19 letters, 1823–1830.
Catton collection, Derby Borough Library.

ARTHUR YOUNG, four letters, 1815–1819.
B.M. Add. MSS. 35132–35133.

Printed Material

Travel Diaries of Thomas Robert Malthus, ed. Patricia James (Cambridge, 1966).

Mrs James has in preparation a biography of Malthus using a wide range of manuscript material, of which the above list represents only the most sizeable and/or economically interesting groups.

GEORGE F. MCCLEARY, *The Malthusian Population Theory* (London, 1953).

Reprints Malthus's published correspondence with Senior.

Palgrave II 668; *DNB* XII 886; *ESS* X 68; *ESS* IX 549.

Portrait: N.P.G. (A).

ALFRED MARSHALL, 1842–1924

17 boxes of notes, lectures and some other material, relating to the whole of Marshall's career. Also 166 letters to him, 1877–1923, and some of his letters to others, principally Foxwell and Edgeworth.
Marshall papers, Marshall Library, Cambridge.

Correspondents

ERNEST ALFRED BENIANS, nine letters, 1904–1913.
St John's College, Cambridge.

CHARLES BOOTH, four letters, 1901–1916.
Booth papers, London U.L., MS. 797.

SIR ARTHUR LYON BOWLEY, four letters, 1901.
Bowley papers, Royal Statistical Society.[19]

EDWIN CANNAN, 45 letters, 1893–1906.
Cannan collection, L.S.E.

JOHN BATES CLARK, nine letters, 1886–1902.
Clark papers, Columbia U.L., New York.

FRANCIS YSIDRO EDGEWORTH, two letters, 1881.
Edgeworth papers.[7]

CHARLES RYLE FAY, ten letters, 1906–1910.
Miscellaneous letters, Marshall Library, Cambridge.

HERBERT SOMERTON FOXWELL, nine letters, 1899.
Foxwell papers, Baker Library, Harvard University.

SIR ROBERT GIFFEN, three letters, 1895–1904.
Giffen collection, L.S.E.

WILLIAM ALBERT SAMUEL HEWINS, 15 letters, 1893–1902.
Hewins papers, Sheffield U.L.

JOHN KELLS INGRAM, four letters, 1890.
Ingram papers, P.R.O.N.I.

WILLIAM STANLEY JEVONS, two letters, 1875–1879.
Jevons papers, Manchester J.R.U.L.

JOHN MAYNARD KEYNES, Baron Keynes, 39 letters, 1906–1923.
Keynes papers, Marshall Library, Cambridge.

JOHN NEVILLE KEYNES, 117 letters, *c.* 1880–1912.
J. N. Keynes correspondence, Marshall Library, Cambridge.

MACMILLANS, several letters, 1881–1924.
B.M. Add. MS. 55174.

SIMON NEWCOMB, four letters, 1892.
Newcomb papers, Library of Congress.

NICOLAAS GERARD PIERSON, five letters, 1891.
Pierson papers, Municipal University of Amsterdam.

SIR WILLIAM ROTHENSTEIN, two letters, 1908.
Houghton Library, Harvard University.

WILLIAM ROBERT SCOTT, two letters, 1902–1922.
Scott papers, P.R.O.N.I.

EDWIN ROBERT ANDERSON SELIGMAN, 18 letters, 1890–1908.
Seligman papers, Columbia U.L., New York.

LÉON WALRAS, eight letters, 1883–1889.
Fonds Walras, Bibliothèque Cantonale et Universitaire, Lausanne.

KNUT WICKSELL, six letters, 1904–1916.
Wicksell papers, Lund Universitetsbibliotek, Sweden.

Printed Material

Professor J. R. Whitaker of the University of Virginia has in preparation an edition of Marshall's early writings.

A. C. PIGOU, *Memorials of Alfred Marshall* (London, 1925).

MARY PALEY MARSHALL, *What I Remember* (Cambridge, 1947).

A. W. COATS, 'Alfred Marshall and the Early Development of the London School of Economics: Some Unpublished Letters', *Economica* (Nov 1967).

H. W. MCCREADY, 'Alfred Marshall: Some Unpublished Letters', *Culture*, xv (1954) 300.

H. W. MCCREADY, 'Alfred Marshall and Tariff Reform, 1903: Some Unpublished Letters', *Journal of Political Economy*, LXIII (1955) 259.

The above articles print letters to Lujo Brentano, 1889–1905.

DNB 1922–1930, 562; *ESS* x 155; *IESS* x 25.

Portraits: N.P.G.(A); St John's College, Cambridge; see Pigou (above).

HARRIET MARTINEAU, 1802–1876

Over 1000 items of correspondence, almost entirely in-letters, with some manuscript notes, parts of manuscripts of her works, and various printed items.
Harriet Martineau papers, Birmingham U.L.

A small group of in- and out-letters with other documents.
Boston (U.S.A.) Public Library.

A 41-page manuscript entitled 'Health in the Camp', *c.* 1860.
Columbia U.L., New York.

27 single letters between Harriet Martineau and various correspondents, 1832–1869.
Houghton Library, Harvard University.

Correspondents

CHARLES BABBAGE, four letters, n.d.
B.M. Add. MS. 37201.

JOHN BRIGHT, about five letters, 1845–1846.
B.M. Add. MS. 43389.

HENRY PETER BROUGHAM, 1st Baron Brougham and Vaux, 14 letters, 1832–1866.
Brougham papers, U.C.L.

SAMUEL BROWN, several letters, 1857–1874.
N.L.S., MSS. 1889–1890.

EDWARD GEORGE EARLE LYTTON BULWER-LYTTON, Baron Lytton, 16 letters (some modern copies), 1844.
Bulwer-Lytton papers, Hertfordshire R.O.

EDWIN CHADWICK, three letters, n.d.
Chadwick papers, U.C.L.

JOHN CHAPMAN, 22 letters, 1853–1858.
Bodleian, MS. Eng. Lett. d2.

JAMES FREEMAN CLARKE, three letters, 1835–184?
Houghton Library, Harvard University.

RICHARD COBDEN, six letters, 1845–1846.
Cobden papers, West Sussex R.O.

EDWARD DAVIES DAVENPORT, two letters, n.d.
Bromley-Davenport Muniments, Manchester J.R.U.L.

RALPH WALDO EMERSON, ten letters, 1836–1852.
Houghton Library, Harvard University.

HENRY GEORGE GREY, 3rd Earl Grey, eight letters, 1844–1848.
Grey of Howick papers, Durham D.P.

GEORGE JACOB HOLYOAKE, 13 letters, 1851–1859.
B.M. Add. MS. 42726.

GEORGE JACOB HOLYOAKE, four letters, 1850–1857.
Holyoake collection, Co-operative Union Ltd, Manchester.

JOHN GEORGE LAMBTON, 1st Earl of Durham (and Lady Durham), 17 letters, 1833–1838.
Lambton papers, N.R.A. 11184.

EDWARD MOXON, 19 letters, n.d.
Bodleian, MS. Eng. Lett. d2.

FLORENCE NIGHTINGALE, many letters, 1858–1871.
B.M. Add. MS. 45788.

SIR ROBERT PEEL, several items, 1846.
B.M. Add. MS. 40585.

FRANCIS PLACE, several items, 1832–1834.
B.M. Add. MS. 35149.

HENRY CRABB ROBINSON, nine letters, 1837–1850.
Crabb Robinson papers, Dr Williams' Library, London.

JACOB SNIDER, three letters, 1844.
Madeira Vaughan collection, American Philosophical Society Library, Philadelphia.

CHARLES SUMNER, three letters, 1839.
Houghton Library, Harvard University.

WILLIAM TAIT, 11 letters, 1832–1837.
Miscellaneous manuscripts, U.C.L.

JOHN HAMILTON THOM, five letters, 1867.
Rathbone papers, Liverpool U.L.

TICKNOR and FIELDS, three letters, 1861.
Houghton Library, Harvard University.

Printed Material

ROBERT K. WEBB, *Harriet Martineau: A Radical Victorian* (London, 1960).

VERA WHEATLEY, *The Life and Work of Harriet Martineau* (London, 1957).

Palgrave II 703; *DNB* XII 1194; Boase II 776; *ESS* X 168.

Portraits: B.M. (P); N.P.G.; see Webb and Wheatley (above).

HERMAN MERIVALE, 1806–1874

The Merivale family papers do not include anything of Herman's. His papers are presumed to have been lost, perhaps as a result of the confused financial affairs of his son, Herman Charles Merivale.

Correspondents

EDWARD GEORGE EARLE LYTTON BULWER-LYTTON, Baron Lytton, several letters, 1857–1863.
Bulwer-Lytton papers, Hertfordshire R.O.

HENRY PELHAM CLINTON, 5th Duke of Newcastle, several letters, 1859–1863.
Newcastle MSS., Nottingham U.L.

ROBERT ARTHUR TALBOT GASCOYNE-CECIL, 3rd Marquess of Salisbury, five letters, 1866–1867.
Salisbury papers, Christ Church College, Oxford.

HENRY GEORGE GREY, 3rd Earl Grey, five letters, 1847–1860.
Grey of Howick papers, Durham D.P.

MACVEY NAPIER, 23 letters, 1835–1847.
B.M. Add. MSS. 34617–34626.

CHARLES ELIOT NORTON, three letters, n.d.
Houghton Library, Harvard University.

JOHN GORHAM PALFREY, five letters, 1856–1865.
Houghton Library, Harvard University.

SIR HENRY JAMES SUMNER-MAINE, 26 letters, 1865–1869.
Sumner-Maine papers, India Office Library.

EDWARD TURNER BOYD TWISLETON, three letters, 1867–1868.
Houghton Library, Harvard University.

Printed Material

ANNA MERIVALE, *Family Memorials* (1884).

Palgrave II 736; *DNB* XIII 280; Boase II 850; *ESS* x 353.

Portrait: N.P.G.(A).

JAMES MILL, 1773–1836

Four volumes of commonplace books, containing extracts on political and philosophical subjects, with his comments, *c.* 1810–1819.
London Library.

One volume of manuscript notes, largely bibliographical. Also two letters of 1831 and 1833 to Albany Fonblanque.
Mill–Taylor collection, L.S.E.

57 letters from David Ricardo, 1811–1823, are kept with the Ricardo papers.
Cambridge U.L., Add. MS. 7510.

Four letters to various correspondents, 1827–1829.
Hollander collection, University of Illinois Library, Urbana.

Some of his correspondence, including letters from Bentham.
John Stuart Mill collection, Yale U.L.

Correspondents

JEREMY BENTHAM, four letters, 1809.
B.M. Add. MS. 33544.

JEREMY BENTHAM, some letters and other papers, 1814–1827.
Bentham papers, U.C.L.

JEREMY BENTHAM, one letter, 1814.
King's College, Cambridge.

HENRY PETER BROUGHAM, 1st Baron Brougham and Vaux, 24 letters, 1811–1836.
Brougham papers, U.C.L.

ARCHIBALD CONSTABLE, four letters, 1825.
N.L.S., MS. 673.

ETIENNE DUMONT, several letters, n.d.
Dumont MSS., Bibliothèque Publique et Universitaire de Genève.

MACVEY NAPIER, 23 letters, 1814–1831.
B.M. Add. MSS. 34611–34615.

FRANCIS PLACE, many items (mainly copies), 1814–1831.
B.M. Add. MSS. 35144–35153, 37949.

DAVID RICARDO, 49 letters, 1810–1823.
Cambridge U.L., Add. MS. 7510.

SIR ROBERT JOHN WILMOT-HORTON, eight letters, 1829–1831.
Catton collection, Derby Borough Library.

Printed Material

ALEXANDER BAIN, *James Mill: A Biography* (London, 1882).

DONALD WINCH, *James Mill: Selected Economic Writings* (Edinburgh, 1966).

Palgrave II 755; *DNB* XIII 382; *ESS* X 480.

Portrait: see Winch (above).

JOHN STUART MILL, 1806–1873

Correspondence, 1822–1873, including Mill's own letters to Fawcett and Cairnes, with many notebooks, accounts and other papers.
Mill–Taylor collection, L.S.E.

Correspondence, 1812–1873, including 237 of his own letters, many of which are to Harriet Taylor, and nearly 200 in-letters, several of which are from economists. Also a journal of a walking tour in Berkshire, Buckinghamshire and Surrey, and some other miscellaneous manuscript items.
J. S. Mill collection, Yale U.L.

Six bound volumes of correspondence, five being in-letters from correspondents including Jeremy Bentham, and one being letters from Mill to various correspondents.
Johns Hopkins U.L., Baltimore.

A group of letters, mostly in his hand, appearing to be drafts of letters to various correspondents, 1840–1863.
Brotherton collection, Leeds U.L.

A collection of his letters to various correspondents, 1829–1859.
King's College, Cambridge.

A manuscript of Mill's *Autobiography*, 230 pages long, and nine letters to various correspondents, 1834–1867.
Hollander collection, University of Illinois Library, Urbana.

A manuscript of *Principles of Political Economy*.
Pierpont Morgan Library, New York.

Other locations for Mill manuscripts (including a press-copy holograph manuscript of the *Logic*, B.M.; a press-copy manuscript of the *Autobiography*, Manchester J.R.U.L.; a holograph manuscript of the *Autobiography*, Columbia U.L., New York) are numerous and details can be obtained from *Collected Works* and the *Mill Newsletter*.

Printed Material

Earlier Letters of John Stuart Mill, 1812–1848, ed. Francis E. Mineka, 2 vols. (Toronto, 1963).

Later Letters of John Stuart Mill, 1849–1873, ed. Francis E. Mineka and Dwight N. Lindley, 4 vols. (Toronto, 1972).

These two collections form vols. 12–13 and 14–17, respectively, of the *Collected Works of John Stuart Mill*, which include other manuscripts in vols. 3 and 8. The volumes of correspondence include Mill's letters only.

Discoveries of Mill manuscripts are regularly noted in the *Mill Newsletter* edited by Professor J. M. Robson of Toronto.

Palgrave II 756; *DNB* XIII 390; Boase II 875; *ESS* X 481; *IESS* X 340.

Portraits: B.M. (P); N.P.G.; City Hall, Westminster.

JOHN MILLAR, 1735–1801

Millar's papers are said to have been destroyed by a descendant *c.* 1943: see Lehmann (below).

18 sets of notes from his lectures on various subjects.
Glasgow U.L.

Two sets of lecture notes on civil law, and one on government.
N.L.S., MSS. 2743, 3930, 3931.

A two-volume set of lecture notes on institutions of civil law, 1794.
Edinburgh U.L.

A set of notes from his lectures on government, 1782.
Aberdeen U.L.

Correspondents

WILLIAM ADAM, several letters, 1784–1799.
Adam papers, N.R.A. 9954.

EDMUND BURKE, four letters, 1784–1785.
Wentworth Woodhouse Muniments, Sheffield City Library.

EDMUND BURKE, one letter, 1784.
Fitzwilliam MSS., Northamptonshire R.O.

DAVID DOUGLAS, two letters, 1790.
Bannerman collection, Glasgow U.L.

DAVID HUME, one letter, *c.* 1776.
Hume papers, Royal Society of Edinburgh.

WILLIAM PITT the Younger, three letters, n.d.
Chatham papers, P.R.O.

ADAM SMITH, one letter, 1764.
Bannerman collection, Glasgow U.L.

Printed Material

W. C. LEHMANN, *John Millar of Glasgow, 1735–1801* (Glasgow, 1960).

Palgrave II 764; *DNB* XIII 401; *IESS* X 348.

Portraits: N.P.G. (A); see Lehmann (above).

WILLIAM NEWMARCH, 1820–1882

Various manuscript and printed papers, including notes for papers on political economy, 1866–1882; correspondence on the British Association and the Social Science Association, 1856–1862; and letters from his own son, W. J. Newmarch, 1859–1865.
Newmarch papers, Royal Statistical Society.[19]

The records of the Globe Insurance Company, 1851–1862, include letters and memoranda by Newmarch.
Guildhall Library, MSS. 11656–11685, 11694.

Correspondents
JOHN ELLIOT CAIRNES, three letters, 1858–1862.
N.L.I., MS. 8944.

SIR ROBERT HARRY INGLIS PALGRAVE, four letters, 1871–1874.
Palgrave papers.[9]

JAMES EDWIN THOROLD ROGERS, five letters, 1859–1881.
Thorold Rogers papers, N.R.A. 12396.

JOHN STRANG, 17 letters, 1854–1861.
Records of the Dilettante Society of Glasgow, Glasgow City Archives.

Printed Material
Palgrave III 17; *DNB* XIV 352; Boase II 1125; *ESS* XI 368.

JOSEPH SHIELD NICHOLSON, 1850–1927

Nicholson's daughter has no papers, and none are known elsewhere.

Correspondents
WILLIAM BLACKWOOD & SONS, letters to and from, 1888–1893.
N.L.S., MSS. 4522, 4539, 4605, 4725.

EDWIN CANNAN, 20 letters, 1904–1925.
Cannan collection, L.S.E.

FRANCIS YSIDRO EDGEWORTH, two letters, 1888–1891.
Edgeworth papers.[7]

CHARLES RYLE FAY, six letters, 1908–1910.
Miscellaneous letters, Marshall Library, Cambridge.

SIR ARCHIBALD GEIKIE, three letters, 1891–1892.
Edinburgh U.L.

JOHN NEVILLE KEYNES, 24 letters, 1884–1909.
J. N. Keynes correspondence, Marshall Library, Cambridge.

SIR ROBERT HARRY INGLIS PALGRAVE, four letters, 1886–1897.
Palgrave papers.[9]

EDWIN ROBERT ANDERSON SELIGMAN, two letters, 1896–1910.
Seligman papers, Columbia U.L., New York.

Printed Material

WILLIAM ROBERT SCOTT, 'Joseph Shield Nicholson, 1850–1927', *Proceedings of the British Academy*, XIV (1928).

DNB 1922–1930, 635.

Portrait: N.P.G. (A).

ROBERT OWEN, 1771–1858

Correspondence, consisting of nearly 3000 items, mainly letters to Owen, 1821–1858, but including a few drafts and copies of out-letters and other documents.
Owen papers, Co-operative Union Ltd, Manchester.

A small group of letters (about ten) to Owen, 1830–1858, and about 70 typescript copies of letters and parts of letters, 1822–1851.
N.L.W., MSS. 14352, 18894.

Two letters, a scrapbook containing manuscript material and a draft of the *Report to the County of Lanark*, *c.* 1818–1820.
London U.L., A.L.s 146 and 266, MSS. 578 and 692.

His diary, 1813–1822, and business records of his period at New Lanark.
Gourock Ropeworks Co. papers, N.R.A. 10832.

Correspondence, financial and other records of Owen and the New Harmony Community, 1824–1829, including many Owen family papers.
Workingmen's Institute, New Harmony, Indiana.

Minute book of the Central Board of the Association of All Classes of All Nations, 1838–1840. Minute book of the Directors of the National Community Friendly Society, 1838–1843. Minute book of the Directors of the Rational Society, 1843–1845.
International Institute of Social History, Amsterdam.

Correspondents

THOMAS ALLSOP, *c.* 150 letters, 1832–1858.
B.M. Add. MS. 46344.

JEREMY BENTHAM, nine letters, 1818–1823.
B.M. Add. MS. 33545.

HENRY PETER BROUGHAM, 1st Baron Brougham and Vaux, 40 letters, 1833–1858.
Brougham papers, U.C.L.

JAMES M. DORSEY, four letters, 1827–1828.
Dorsey–Owen papers, Indiana Historical Society, Indianapolis.

PHILIPP EMANUEL VON FELLENBERG, 20 letters (from Owen and his sons), 1818–1835.
Fellenberg MSS., Burgerbibliothek, Berne.

ARCHIBALD JAMES HAMILTON, one letter, 1828.
Hamilton papers, Motherwell Public Library.

ROBERT BANKS JENKINSON, 2nd Earl of Liverpool, nine items, 1818–1820.
B.M. Add. MSS. 38271–38574.

SAMUEL OLDKNOW, two letters, 1793.
N.L.W., MS. 4956.

SIR ROBERT PEEL, six items, 1822–1846.
B.M. Add. MSS. 40349–40588.

SIR ROBERT JOHN WILMOT-HORTON, two letters, 1831.
Catton collection, Derby Borough Library.

Printed Material

J. M. ELLIOTT, 'The Owen Family Papers', *Indiana Magazine of History*, LX 4 (1964).

J. F. C. HARRISON, *Robert Owen and the Owenites* (London, 1969).

Palgrave III 46; *DNB* XIV 1338; Boase II 1291; *ESS* XI 517; *IESS* XI 351.

Portraits: B.M.(P); N.P.G.; S.N.P.G.; Courtauld Institute.

SIR ROBERT HARRY INGLIS PALGRAVE, 1827–1919

The Palgrave family papers contain much correspondence of Sir Inglis with other members of the family, 1847–1903, as well

as five bundles of correspondence with economists and bankers (mainly 1880s and 1890s) and a few other papers relating to him.
Palgrave papers.[9]

A group of 27 letters to Palgrave, 1873–1882.
King's College, Cambridge.

Journal of a tour in France, 1847.
B.M. Add. MS. 45738.

Correspondents

EDWIN CANNAN, 44 letters, 1890–1917.
Cannan collection, L.S.E.

JOHN BATES CLARK, three letters, 1891.
Clark papers, Columbia U.L., New York.

FRANCIS YSIDRO EDGEWORTH, two letters, 1888–1891.
Edgeworth papers.[7]

HERBERT SOMERTON FOXWELL, three letters, 1899.
Foxwell papers, Baker Library, Harvard University.

JOHN KELLS INGRAM, 16 letters, 1888–1899.
Ingram papers, P.R.O.N.I.

WILLIAM STANLEY JEVONS, four letters, 1873–1876.
Jevons papers, Manchester J.R.U.L.

JOHN NEVILLE KEYNES, 63 letters, 1886–1917.
J. N. Keynes correspondence, Marshall Library, Cambridge.

SIR WILLIAM LEE-WARNER, two letters, 1881.
Lee-Warner MSS., India Office Library.

ALFRED MILNER, 1st Viscount Milner, four letters, 1884–1889.
Welby collection, L.S.E.

EDWIN ROBERT ANDERSON SELIGMAN, 18 letters, 1892–1909.
Seligman papers, Columbia U.L., New York.

Printed Material

ESS XI 536.

HENRY BROOKE PARNELL, 1st BARON CONGLETON, 1778–1842

Personal and political papers, 1785–1842, including much correspondence from politicians and economists. Also commonplace books (which contain accounts of Political Economy Club meetings) and other papers.
Congleton papers.[12]

Correspondents

HENRY PETER BROUGHAM, 1st Baron Brougham and Vaux, 13 letters, 1812–1834.
Brougham papers, U.C.L.

WILLIAM HUSKISSON, three items, 1827.
B.M. Add. MS. 38751.

ROBERT BANKS JENKINSON, 2nd Earl of Liverpool, four items, 1814–1820.
B.M. Add. MSS. 38257–38379.

MACVEY NAPIER, 15 letters, 1840–1841.
B.M. Add. MSS. 34621–34622.

SIR ROBERT PEEL, 11 items, 1813–1829.
B.M. Add. MSS. 40226–40399.

THOMAS TELFORD, 16 letters, 1819–1827.
Telford papers, Institution of Civil Engineers, London.

Printed Material

Palgrave III 64; *DNB* xv 342.

JAMES PENNINGTON, 1777–1862

No Pennington papers are known to exist.

The so-called Pennington Papers of the University of Chicago Library are in fact three out-letters and one in-letter, 1845–1862, to Treasury officials on financial matters.

One letter of W. E. Gladstone to Pennington, 1854.
London U.L., A.L. 54.

Correspondents

GEORGE ARBUTHNOT, letters and memoranda, 1827–1855.
Welby collection, L.S.E.

WILLIAM EWART GLADSTONE, a memorandum, n.d.
B.M. Add. MS. 44580.

WILLIAM HUSKISSON, three letters, 1827.
B.M. Add. MS. 38749.

SIR ROBERT PEEL, 16 letters, 1827–1850.
B.M. Add. MSS. 40543–40610.

SIR CHARLES EDWARD TREVELYAN, a memo and letter, 1841.
Goulburn papers, Surrey R.O.

SIR ROBERT JOHN WILMOT-HORTON, 13 letters, 1828–1831.
Catton collection, Derby Borough Library.

CHARLES WOOD, 1st Viscount Halifax, one letter, 1843.
Grey of Howick papers, Durham D.P.

Printed Material

Economic Writings of James Pennington, ed. Richard S. Sayers (London, 1963).

Palgrave III 82; *DNB* XV 555; Boase II 1454.

ARTHUR CECIL PIGOU, 1877–1959

A fellowship dissertation of 1902, 'Causes and Effects of Changes in the Relative Values of Agricultural Produce in the U.K. During the Last Fifty Years'.
King's College, Cambridge.

Some printed and typed papers resulting from his work on the Committee on Currency and Bank of England Note Issues.
Marshall Library, Cambridge.

Correspondents

WILLIAM HENRY BEVERIDGE, Baron Beveridge, several letters, 1924–1941.
Beveridge papers, L.S.E.

EDWIN CANNAN, 26 letters, 1914–1933.
Cannan collection, L.S.E.

COLIN CLARK, three letters and a memo, 1937–1939.
Clark papers.[13]

JOHN MAYNARD KEYNES, Baron Keynes, 56 letters, mostly n.d.
Keynes papers, Marshall Library, Cambridge.

JOHN MAYNARD KEYNES, Baron Keynes, 25 letters, n.d.
Keynes papers, King's College, Cambridge.

MACMILLANS, many letters, 1904–1956.
B.M. Add. MSS. 55199, 55200.

Printed Material

JOHN SALTMARSH AND PATRICK WILKINSON, *Arthur Cecil Pigou, 1877–1959: Fellow and Professor of Political Economy* (Cambridge, 1960).

DNB 1951–1960, 814; *IESS* XII 90.

Portraits: N.P.G. (A); Marshall Library, Cambridge.

FRANCIS PLACE, 1771–1854

Manuscripts and working papers of books.
B.M. Add. MSS. 27789–27859.

The manuscript of Place's autobiography, with correspondence and other papers.
B.M. Add. MSS. 35142–35154.

Commonplace books, 1775–1844.
B.M. Add. MSS. 36623–36628.

Letters to Place, 1813–1852.
B.M. Add. MSS. 37949–37950.

Place's collection of newspaper cuttings, in 180 volumes, contains some manuscript letters.
B.M. Dept. of Printed Books.

Five letters to and from Place, 1823–1838.
London U.L., A.L.s 99, 100, 251, 252, 356.

Several letters from Place to different correspondents, 1840.
Ely collection, Louisiana State U.L., Baton Rouge.

A six-page manuscript of 'Remarks upon Mr Ricardo's Observations'.
Seligman collection, Columbia U.L., New York.

Correspondents

HENRY PETER BROUGHAM, 1st Baron Brougham and Vaux, 36 letters, 1831–1852.
Brougham papers, U.C.L.

EDWIN CHADWICK, eight letters, 1829–1841.
Chadwick papers, U.C.L.

RICHARD COBDEN, four letters, 1840–1849.
B.M. Add. MSS. 43667–43668.

JOHN CAM HOBHOUSE, 1st Baron Broughton, *c.* 150 items, 1818–1831.
B.M. Add. MSS. 36457–36466.

GEORGE JACOB HOLYOAKE, four letters, 1842–1850.
Holyoake collection, Co-operative Union Ltd, Manchester.

ROBERT OWEN, three letters, 1831–1838.
Owen correspondence, Co-operative Union Ltd, Manchester.

JOSEPH PARKES, five letters, 1851–1853.
Parkes papers, U.C.L.

GEORGE JOHN SPENCER, 2nd Earl Spencer, three letters, 1822.
Spencer papers, N.R.A. 10410.

SAMUEL WHITBREAD, two letters, 1813.
Whitbread papers, Bedfordshire R.O.

SIR ROBERT JOHN WILMOT-HORTON, five items, 1830.
Catton collection, Derby Borough Library.

Printed Material

Autobiography of Francis Place, ed. Mary Thale (London, 1972).

London Radicalism, 1830–1843: A Selection from the Papers of Francis Place, ed. D. J. Rowe (London, 1970).

GRAHAM WALLAS, *Life of Francis Place* (London, 1898).

Palgrave III 112; *DNB* XV 1276; Boase II 1552; *ESS* XII 143.

Portraits: N.P.G.; see *Autobiography* (above).

GEORGE RICHARDSON PORTER, 1792–1852

Letters and reports connected with his Board of Trade work, particularly Anglo-French commercial negotiations, 1839–1847.
Bodleian, MS. Clar. Dep. c469, c545, c547.

The letter books of the Board of Trade, and its Statistical Section, contain copies of many letters sent by Porter on official business.
P.R.O.

Correspondents

CHARLES BABBAGE, four letters, 1834–1842.
B.M. Add. MSS. 37188–37192.

SIR JOHN FREDERICK WILLIAM HERSCHEL, five letters, 1848–1849.
Herschel papers, Royal Society Library, London.

SIR ROBERT PEEL, six items, 1840–1846.
B.M. Add. MSS. 40493.

ADOLPHE QUÉTELET, 20 letters, 1835–1851.
Quételet papers, Bibliothèque Royale de Belgique, Brussels.

GEORGE WILLIAM FREDERICK VILLIERS, 4th Earl of Clarendon, six letters, 1840–1846.
Bodleian, MS. Clar. Dep. c545, c547.

GEORGE WILSON, two letters, 1841–1852.
Wilson papers, Manchester City Library.

Printed Material

Palgrave III 170; *DNB* XVI 178; Boase II 1591.

Portrait: Royal Statistical Society.

BONAMY PRICE, 1807–1888

Price's papers have not been traced.

Correspondents
ARTHUR HUGH CLOUGH, about six letters, 1845–1852.
Bodleian, MS. Eng. Lett. c190, d175, d177.

WILLIAM EWART GLADSTONE, 19 items, 1834–1882.
B.M. Add. MSS. 44353–44477.

ROUNDELL PALMER, 1st Earl of Selborne, two letters, 1864–1874.
Selborne papers, Lambeth Palace Library, London.

WILLIAM RATHBONE, two letters, 1864.
Rathbone papers, Liverpool U.L.

CAMPBELL TAIT, Archbishop of Canterbury, 13 letters, 1842–1882.
Tait papers, Lambeth Palace Library, London.

Printed Material
Palgrave III 188; *DNB* XVI 322; Boase II 1635.

Portrait: Worcester College, Oxford.

RICHARD PRICE, 1723–1791

Letters to and from Price, 1767–1790, on politics and other topics, 113 in number.
American Philosophical Society Library, Philadelphia.

38 letters to Price, 1753–1791, the largest groups being from Joseph Priestley and Lord Lansdowne.
Bodleian, MS. Eng. Misc. c132.

A bound volume containing copies of Price's letters to John Edwards, actuary of the Equitable Assurance Society, with actuarial calculations, 1768–1771. A 31-page manuscript of observations on the keeping of the Society's accounts, 1775.
Archives of the Equitable Life Assurance Society.[15]

Manuscripts on a wide variety of economic topics, mostly

undated, and intended for the information of William Petty, Marquess of Lansdowne.
Shelburne papers, W. L. Clements Library, University of Michigan, Ann Arbor.

Correspondents
JOHN CANTON, two letters, 1764–1768.
Royal Society Library, London.

ALEXANDER CHRISTIE, copies of letters, 1790.
N.L.S., MS. 3703.

BENJAMIN FRANKLIN, 23 letters, 1766–1788.
Franklin papers, American Philosophical Society Library, Philadelphia.

WILLIAM PETTY, 1st Marquess of Lansdowne, many letters, 1771–1790.
Lansdowne papers, H.M.C. 6th Rept.

WILLIAM PITT, 1st Earl of Chatham, seven letters, 1772–1775.
Chatham papers, P.R.O.

WILLIAM PITT the Younger, six letters, 1784–1786.
Chatham papers, P.R.O.

EZRA STYLES, several letters, 1778–1790.
Yale U.L.

Printed Material
Dr D. O. Thomas, Dept. of Philosophy, University College of Wales, Aberystwyth, has in preparation a comprehensive edition of Price's correspondence.

Palgrave III 189; *DNB* XVI 334; *ESS* XII 350.

Portraits: B.M. (P); N.P.G. (A); New College, London.

DAVID RICARDO, 1772–1823

Correspondence received, with a few copies of out-letters. Includes much correspondence with economists, but also letters on estate, family, business and club affairs. Commonplace books, notes, a continental tour journal and the manuscripts of

some works not published in his lifetime. (Kept with these are his letters to Malthus, Mill and Wilkinson.)
Ricardo papers, Cambridge U.L., Add. MS. 7510.

A bound volume of letters to members of the Ricardo family, on financial matters, 32 items, 1819–1843. Items 1–7 are to David Ricardo, 1819–1823, and several of the others deal with his estate.
Ricardo papers, L.S.E.

Printed Material

Works and Correspondence of David Ricardo, ed. Piero Sraffa, 11 vols. (London, 1951–1973).
Vols. 6–9 are Ricardo's complete economic correspondence.

Palgrave III 304; *DNB* XVI 979; *ESS* XIII 378; *IESS* XIII 507.

Portraits: B.M.(P); N.P.G.(A); see *Works and Correspondence* (above).

JAMES EDWIN THOROLD ROGERS, 1823–1890

Nearly 800 itmes of correspondence, 1854–1890, all but a few in-letters, with one or two other papers. Some of the correspondence with economists.
Thorold Rogers papers, N.R.A. 12396.

Correspondents

GEORGE BENTLEY, several letters, 1872–1880.
Bodleian, MS. Eng. Lett. d100.

EDWIN CHADWICK, two letters, n.d.
Chadwick papers, U.C.L.

RICHARD COBDEN, ten letters, 1857–1865.
B.M. Add. MSS. 43669, 43671.

RICHARD THEODORE ELY, two or three letters, 1880s.
Ely papers, University of Wisconsin Library, Madison.

WILLIAM EWART GLADSTONE, 34 items, 1854–1889.
B.M. Add. MSS. 44379–44506.

GEORGE JACOB HOLYOAKE, 12 letters, 1868–1890.
Holyoake collection, Co-operative Union Ltd, Manchester.

WILLIAM STANLEY JEVONS, three letters, 1863–1866.
Jevons papers, Manchester J.R.U.L.

Printed Material
Palgrave III 319; *DNB* XVII 123; Boase III 258; *ESS* XIII 417, *IESS* XIII 542.

Portrait: Worcester College, Oxford.

GEORGE ROSE, 1744–1818

Papers, including much correspondence, mainly from the latter part of his life.
B.M. Add. MSS. 42772–42780.

Rose family papers, including two volumes of letters of George Rose, 1776–1817, on personal, family and official business.
N.L.S., MSS. 3795–3801.

Letters to Rose from Hugh Hume Campbell, 3rd Earl of Marchmont, 1773–1793.
N.L.S., MS. 3523.

Correspondents
WILLIAM ADAM, about five letters, 1795–1802.
Adam papers, N.R.A. 9954.

WILLIAM DACRES ADAMS, nine items, 1800–1809.
Adams papers, P.R.O.

SIR JOSEPH BANKS, three letters, 1789–1791.
B.M. Add. MSS. 33978–33982.

JEREMY BENTHAM, 26 items, 1792–1801.
B.M. Add. MSS. 33541–33543.

JEREMY BENTHAM, more letters and other papers, 1791–1799.
Bentham papers, U.C.L.

CHARLES BLAGDEN, nine letters, 1791–1792.
Blagden papers, Royal Society Library, London.

GEORGE CANNING, many letters, 1802–1815.
Canning papers, Leeds City Library, Archives Dept.

SIR HENRY CLINTON, 20 items, 1783–1792.
Clinton papers, W. L. Clements Library, University of Michigan, Ann Arbor.

JOHN WILSON CROKER, 60 letters, 1810–1817.
Croker papers, W. L. Clements Library, University of Michigan, Ann Arbor.

HENRY DUNDAS, 1st Viscount Melville, *c.* 40 items, 1789–1816.
N.L.S., MS. 18.

WILLIAM EDEN, 1st Baron Auckland, *c.* 150 items, 1785–1806.
B.M. Add. MSS. 34420–34461.

JOHN FOSTER, 1st Baron Oriel, five items, 1809.
Foster/Massereene papers, P.R.O.N.I.

HENRY MACKENZIE, 18 letters, 1800–1811.
N.L.S., MS. 6371.

HORATIO NELSON, 1st Viscount Nelson, nine items, 1793–1805.
B.M. Add. MSS. 34902–34931.

THOMAS ORDE, Baron Bolton, several letters, 1784–1787.
Bolton papers, N.L.I.

SIR ROBERT PEEL, six letters, 1814–1817.
B.M. Add. MSS. 40236–40268.

WILLIAM PITT the Younger, 58 letters, n.d.
Chatham papers, P.R.O.

GEORGE JOHN SPENCER, 2nd Earl Spencer, six letters, 1800–1817.
Spencer papers, N.R.A. 10410.

NICHOLAS VANSITTART, Baron Bexley, three items, 1809–1815.
B.M. Add. MSS. 31231, 31237.

WILLIAM WILBERFORCE, four letters, 1784–1800.
Bodleian, MS. Wilberforce.

THOMAS WILLIS, five letters, 1801.
B.M. Add. MS. 41694.

PHILIP YORKE, 3rd Earl of Hardwicke, five letters, 1788–1802.
B.M. Add. MSS. 35641–35737.

ARTHUR YOUNG, 11 items, 1785–1816.
B.M. Add. MSS. 35126–35128.

Printed Material

L. V. HARCOURT, *The Diaries and Correspondence of the Right Hon. George Rose*, 2 vols. (London, 1860).

Palgrave III 327; *DNB* XVII 226.

Portrait: N.P.G.

WILLIAM ROBERT SCOTT, 1868–1940

Seven boxes of papers, mainly connected with his work on Adam Smith and including copies of Smith letters and papers from various sources. There is also correspondence and manuscripts of books and papers, mainly from the 1930s.
Scott papers, Glasgow U.L.

Scott family papers, including estate accounts, a group of 59 letters to Scott, 1891–1935, and MSS. of historical work on Ireland.
P.R.O.N.I.

Records of Scott's administrative work at the University of St Andrews.
St Andrews University Archives.

Correspondents

EDWIN CANNAN, 11 letters, 1905–1935.
Cannan collection, L.S.E.

ARTHUR H. COLE (and Wallace B. Donham), 80 letters, 1929–1940.
Baker Library Archives, Harvard University.

JOHN MAYNARD KEYNES, Baron Keynes, 28 letters, 1915–1938.
Keynes papers, Marshall Library, Cambridge.

SIR D'ARCY WENTWORTH THOMPSON, four letters, 1907.
Thompson papers, St Andrews U.L.

Printed Material

JOHN H. CLAPHAM, 'William Robert Scott, 1868–1940', *Proceedings of the British Academy,* XXVII (1941).

Portrait: see Clapham (above).

GEORGE POULETT SCROPE, 1797–1876

Scrope left his papers to his nephew, Hugh Hammersley, but the Hammersley family no longer has them. See reference in the C. E. P. Thomson list.

Genealogical material on the family of Scrope, including one volume of notes by Poulett Scrope.
B.M. Add. MSS. 28205–28213.

A ten-page memorandum on parochial assessments, 1861.
N.L.W., Harpton Court papers, 3689.

Correspondents

EDWIN CHADWICK, nine letters, 1837–1859.
Chadwick papers, U.C.L.

JAMES DAVID FORBES, four letters, 1847–1858.
Forbes papers, St Andrews U.L.

WILLIAM EWART GLADSTONE, four letters, 1867–1874.
B.M. Add. MSS. 44412–44442.

HENRY GEORGE GREY, 3rd Earl Grey, four letters, 1831.
Grey of Howick papers, Durham D.P.

SIR CHARLES LYELL, two letters, 1859–1872.
American Philosophical Society Library, Philadelphia.

SIR ROBERT PEEL, three letters, 1838–1849.
B.M. Add. MSS. 40425–40602.

LORD JOHN RUSSELL, 1st Earl Russell, two items, 1848.
Russell papers, P.R.O.

HENRY JOHN TEMPLE, 3rd Viscount Palmerston, two letters, 1841–1848.
Broadlands papers, N.R.A. 12889.

Printed Material

Palgrave III 369; *DNB* XVII 1073; Boase III 465; *ESS* XIII 610.

Portraits: *Geological Magazine* (1870) 193; Archibald Geikie, *Life of Sir Roderick I. Murchison*, 2 vols. (London, 1875).

NASSAU WILLIAM SENIOR, 1790–1864

Correspondence, tour journals, lecture notes, memoranda and other papers on Poor Laws, the Irish Question and numerous other aspects of his interests, and from the whole period of his life. Also family papers from before and biographical materials from after his life.
Nassau Senior papers, N.L.W.

Six volumes of journal, 1853–1863, of tours mainly in France.
Bodleian, MS. Eng. Hist. d245–d247, d259–d260, d262.

17 volumes of journal, 1855–1863.
Bristol U.L.

An account of the Poor Law Amendment Bill conference of 1834.
London U.L., MS. 173.

Correspondents

CHARLES BABBAGE, four letters, 1836.
B.M. Add. MSS. 37189–37201.

JOSEPH HEKEKYAN BEY, seven letters, 1856–1862.
B.M. Add. MS. 37463.

HENRY PETER BROUGHAM, 1st Baron Brougham and Vaux, 27 letters, 1831–1861.
Brougham papers, U.C.L.

EDWIN CHADWICK, six items, 1834–1845.
Chadwick papers, U.C.L.

HENRY RICHARD VASSALL FOX, 3rd Baron of Holland, 21 letters, 1851–1867.
B.M. Add. MS. 52021.

WILLIAM EWART GLADSTONE, four letters, 1851–1854.
B.M. Add. MSS. 44370–44382.

GEORGE HAMILTON GORDON, 4th Earl of Aberdeen, three letters, 1842–1859.
B.M. Add. MSS. 43239, 43255.

HENRY GEORGE GREY, 3rd Earl Grey, four letters, 1836–1853.
Grey of Howick papers, Durham D.P.

SAMUEL JONES LOYD, Baron Overstone, two letters, 1840–1852.
Overstone papers, London U.L., MS. 804.

MACVEY NAPIER, 65 letters, 1841–1847.
B.M. Add. MSS. 34261–34266.

JOHN GORHAM PALFREY, two letters, 1856–1860.
Houghton Library, Harvard University.

JOSEPH PARKES, two letters, 1854.
Parkes papers, U.C.L.

ADOLPHE QUÉTELET, 30 letters, 1831–1851.
Quételet papers, Bibliothèque Royale de Belgique, Brussels.

CHARLES SUMNER, two letters, n.d.
Houghton Library, Harvard University.

CHARLES EDWARD POULETT THOMSON, Baron Sydenham, three letters, 1837.
Grey of Howick papers, Durham D.P.

THOMAS HYDE VILLIERS, two items, 1831.
Bodleian, MS. Clar. Dep. c548.

DANIEL WEBSTER, two letters, 1839.
Houghton Library, Harvard University.

SIR ROBERT JOHN WILMOT-HORTON, 16 letters, 1829–1836.
Catton collection, Derby Borough Library.

Printed Material

MARIAN BOWLEY, *Nassau Senior and Classical Economics* (London, 1937).

SAMUEL L. LEVY, *Nassau W. Senior, 1790–1864* (Newton Abbot, 1970).

NASSAU W. SENIOR, *Industrial Efficiency and Social Economy*, ed. S. L. Levy, 2 vols. (London, 1929).

Palgrave III 377; *DNB* XVII 1183; Boase III 492; *ESS* XIII 662; *IESS* XIV 169.

Portraits: B.M.(P); see Levy (above).

HENRY SIDGWICK, 1838–1900

25 boxes, containing notebooks, lectures, diaries and autobiographical fragments, and correspondence. There are copies of some out-letters, and over 500 letters received by Sidgwick, including some from economists. Also reviews and letters connected with the memoir of Sidgwick published in 1906.
Sidgwick papers, Trinity College, Cambridge.

Notes from his lectures on philosophical topics, 1874–1876, mainly taken by J. N. Keynes.
King's College, Cambridge.

Typed copies of letters from Roden B. W. Noel to Sidgwick, 1861–1878.
Noel papers, Hull U.L.

14 letters from F. W. Maitland to Sidgwick, 1877–1900.
Maitland papers, Cambridge U.L., Add. MS. 7006.

Correspondents

ARTHUR JAMES BALFOUR, 1st Earl of Balfour, 40 letters, 1878–1900.
B.M. Add. MS. 49832.

MARY BENSON, letters to and from, 1857–1900.
Bodleian, MS. Dep. Benson 3.

JAMES BRYCE, Viscount Bryce, 110 items, 1865–1900.
Bryce papers, Bodleian.

EDWARD ROBERT BULWER-LYTTON, Earl Lytton, four letters, 1889–1891.
Bulwer-Lytton papers, Hertfordshire R.O.

FRANCIS YSIDRO EDGEWORTH, three letters, 1882–1887.
Edgeworth papers.[7]

RICHARD THEODORE ELY, one or two letters, 1880s.
Ely papers, University of Wisconsin, Madison.

EDWARD ENFIELD, 18 letters, 1868–1869.
Dr Williams' Library, London.

JOHN NEVILLE KEYNES, four letters, 1891–1900.
J. N. Keynes correspondence, Marshall Library, Cambridge.

JOHN NEVILLE KEYNES, four letters, 1885–1899.
J. N. Keynes correspondence, Cambridge U.L., Add. MS. 7562.

MACMILLANS, several letters, 1866–1896.
B.M. Add. MS. 55159.

FREDERIC WILLIAM HENRY MYERS, ten letters, 1877–1888.
Myers papers, Trinity College, Cambridge.

CHARLES ELIOT NORTON, three letters, n.d.
Houghton Library, Harvard University.

SIR ROBERT HARRY INGLIS PALGRAVE, three letters, 1886–1895.
Palgrave papers.[9]

CHARLES HENRY PEARSON, five letters, 1873–1893.
Bodleian, MS. Eng. Lett. d190.

GEORGE CROOM ROBERTSON, six letters, 1878–1892.
Robertson papers, U.C.L.

HERBERT SPENCER, two letters, 1891–1897.
Spencer papers, London U.L., MS. 791.

JOHN ADDINGTON SYMONDS, six letters, 1882–1890.
Symonds papers, Bristol U.L.

SEDLEY TAYLOR, six letters, 1876–1895.
Cambridge U.L., Add. MS. 6260.

Printed Material

A. SIDGWICK and E. M. SIDGWICK, *Henry Sidgwick: A Memoir* (London, 1906).

DNB XXII 1214; Boase VI 559; *ESS* XIV 48; *IESS* XIV 235.

Portrait: N.P.G.(A).

SIR JOHN SINCLAIR, 1754–1835

Correspondence including draft replies, also estate papers, 1778–1835.
Sinclair of Ulbster papers, N.R.A. 10552. The Scottish Record Office has a microfilm of parts of the Sinclair of Ulbster papers. Mrs Rosalind Mitchison, Dept. of Economic History, Edinburgh University, has transcripts of some other parts.

Papers on the West Indies, 1815–1824.
Bodleian, MS. Clar. Dep. c376.

A group of letters to various correspondents, 1789–1811.
N.L.S., MS. 641.

Some juvenile poems, begun in 1770.
N.L.S., MS. 2253.

A small group of letters, some connected with his work at the Board of Agriculture, 1791–1807.
Reading U.L.

The letter books of the Board of Agriculture, 1793–1798, include many letters sent out in Sinclair's name.
Royal Agricultural Society of England, Kenilworth.

Correspondents

WILLIAM ADAM, about ten letters, 1794–1819.
Adam papers, N.R.A. 9954.

SIR JOSEPH BANKS, 13 letters, 1785–1814.
B.M. Add. MSS. 33978–33982.

SIR JOSEPH BANKS, 13 letters, 1789–1809.
Banks papers, California State Library, Sutro Branch.

HENRY PETER BROUGHAM, 1st Baron Brougham and Vaux, 18 letters, 1825–1835.
Brougham papers, U.C.L.

GEORGE CANNING, several letters, 1822–1827.
Canning papers, Leeds City Library, Archives Dept.

THOMAS CHALMERS, eight letters, 1832.
Chalmers papers, New College, Edinburgh.

ROBERT DOUGLAS, nine letters, 1795–1797.
N.L.S., MSS. 3116–3117.

HENRY DUNDAS, 1st Viscount Melville, and Robert Dundas, 2nd Viscount, six letters, 1793–1828.
N.L.S., MS. 9370.

HENRY DUNDAS, and ROBERT DUNDAS, 22 letters, 1784–1825.
Melville Castle Muniments, Scottish R.O.

JOHN FOSTER, 1st Baron Oriel, 30 items, 1807–1823.
Foster/Massereene papers, P.R.O.N.I.

ROBERT FULKE GREVILLE, five letters, 1794–1808.
B.M. Add. MS. 42072.

CHARLES GREY, 2nd Earl Grey, four letters, 1806–1833.
Grey of Howick papers, Durham D.P.

WARREN HASTINGS, 11 items, 1790–1810.
B.M. Add. MS. 29172.

JOHN JAY, *c.* 20 items, 1794–1816.
Jay papers, Columbia U.L., New York.

CHARLES JENKINSON, 1st Earl of Liverpool, 19 items, 1781–1800.
B.M. Add. MSS. 38219–38421.

ROBERT BANKS JENKINSON, 2nd Earl of Liverpool, 27 items, 1807–1823.
B.M. Add. MSS. 38243–38572.

SIR ROBERT MURRAY KEITH, four letters, 1786–1787.
B.M. Add. MSS. 35537–35538.

SIR ROBERT LISTON, 21 letters, 1821–1830.
N.L.S., MS. 5665.

SIR ROBERT PEEL, 36 letters, 1816–1834.
B.M. Add. MSS. 40261–40407.

WILLIAM PITT the Younger, 50 letters, n.d.
Chatham papers, P.R.O.

DAVID RICARDO, two letters, 1814.
Ricardo papers, Cambridge U.L., MS. 7510.

ROYAL SOCIETY OF ARTS, ten letters, 1794–1819.
Royal Society of Arts Library, London.

SIR WALTER SCOTT, nine letters, 1809–1831.
N.L.S., MS. 3878 *et seq.*

GRIM JONSSON THORKELIN, 18 letters, 1786–1824.
Edinburgh U.L.

SAMUEL WHITBREAD, nine letters, 1810–1813.
Whitbread papers, Bedfordshire R.O.

SIR ROBERT JOHN WILMOT-HORTON, two letters, 1827.
Catton collection, Derby Borough Library.

PHILIP YORKE, 3rd Earl of Hardwicke, 18 letters, 1794–1820.
B.M. Add. MSS. 35642–35735.

ARTHUR YOUNG, *c.* 50 items, 1787–1816.
B.M. Add. MSS. 35126–35133.

Printed Material

The Correspondence of Sir John Sinclair, 2 vols. (Edinburgh, 1831).

ROSALIND MITCHISON, *Agricultural Sir John* (London, 1962).

JOHN SINCLAIR, *Memoirs of the Life of Sir John Sinclair* (Edinburgh, 1837).

Palgrave III 402; *DNB* XVIII 301; *ESS* XIV 62.

Portraits: B.M. (P); N.P.G.; see Mitchison (above).

ADAM SMITH, 1723–1790

Letters to and from Smith, 1740–1790, with fragments of notes, drafts, parts of lectures and also papers of his father.
Bannerman collection, Glasgow U.L.

Notes from his lectures on jurisprudence, 1766. Also various single letters to and from Smith.
Glasgow U.L.

The minutes of the Scottish Customs Board during the period of Smith's membership are in the Scottish Record Office, and there is a collection of relevant letters and accounts, assembled by James Bonar.
Glasgow U.L.

Ten letters to Smith, and five from him, 1775–1776, concerning

the death of David Hume.
Hume MSS., Royal Society of Edinburgh.

Printed Material

WILLIAM ROBERT SCOTT, *Adam Smith as Student and Professor* (Glasgow, 1937).

This includes all the Smith correspondence that was then known. It will be replaced by *The Correspondence of Adam Smith*, edited by E. C. Mossner and I. S. Ross, which is one of a series of volumes devoted to the works of Adam Smith, sponsored by the University of Glasgow, and to be published by the Clarendon Press.

Palgrave III 412; *DNB* XVIII 411; *ESS* XIV 112; *IESS* XIV 322.

Portraits: B.M.(P); N.P.G.; S.N.P.G.

HERBERT SPENCER, 1820–1903

The original manuscripts of most of his works, including a draft of *Social Statics*.
B.M. Add. MSS. 36883–36896, 43831.

148 letters of Spencer to various correspondents on personal and professional matters, 1849–1903.
Knox College Library, Galesburg, Illinois.

Correspondence, 1844–1903, and biographical material on Spencer.
Spencer papers, London U.L., MS. 791.

Six letters to various correspondents, 1863–1891.
American Philosophical Society Library, Philadelphia.

Six letters between Spencer and various correspondents, 1860–1879.
Houghton Library, Harvard University.

Correspondents

CHARLES BABBAGE, seven letters, 1860–1864.
B.M. Add. MSS. 37197–37201.

HENRY HOWE BEMROSE, four letters, 1897–1898.
Derby Borough Library.

SIR JOSEPH EDGAR BOEHM, three letters, 1884.
Darwin collection, University of Virginia Library, Charlottesville.

EDWARD GEORGE EARLE LYTTON BULWER-LYTTON, Baron Lytton, three letters, 1859.
Bulwer-Lytton papers, Hertfordshire R.O.

SIR PERCY BUNTING, 39 letters, 1882–1895.
Bunting papers, University of Chicago Library.

ANDREW CARNEGIE, 44 letters, 1883–1903.
Carnegie papers, Library of Congress.

JOSEPH CHAMBERLAIN, two letters, 1895.
Chamberlain papers, Birmingham U.L.

JOHN CHAPMAN, 9 letters, 1851–1881.
Darwin collection, University of Virginia Library, Charlottesville.

FRANCIS POWER COBBE, five letters, 1866–1875.
Henry E. Huntington Library, San Marino, California.

MONCURE DANIEL CONWAY, four letters, 1872–1900.
Conway papers, Columbia U.L., New York.

JOHN FISKE, 41 letters, 1864–1894.
Henry E. Huntington Library, San Marino, California.

WILLIAM EWART GLADSTONE, 17 items, 1873–1896.
B.M. Add. MSS. 44441–44785.

FREDERIC HARRISON, 20 letters, 1885–1901.
Harrison papers, L.S.E.

ROWLAND G. HAZARD, 13 letters, 1869–1886.
Peacedale collection, Baker Library, Harvard University.

SIR JOHN FREDERICK WILLIAM HERSCHEL, 11 letters, 1859–1865.
Herschel papers, Royal Society Library, London.

GEORGE JACOB HOLYOAKE, 24 letters, 1860–1903.
Holyoake collection, Co-operative Union Ltd, Manchester.

THOMAS HUXLEY, 83 letters, 1851–1900.
Huxley papers, Imperial College, London.

MANTON MARBLE, three letters, 1860–1873.
Marble papers, Library of Congress.

FREDERICK AUGUSTUS MAXSE, typed copies of letters, 1870–1896.
Maxse papers, West Sussex R.O.

JOHN STUART MILL, 24 letters, 1858–1869.
Northwestern U.L., Evanston, Illinois.

JOHN STUART MILL, letter or letters, n.d.
Mill papers, Yale U.L.

STUART RENDEL, 1st Baron Rendel, three letters, 1898–1903.
N.L.W., Rendel papers.

HENRY RICHARD, five letters, 1881–1882.
N.L.W., MS. 5505.

GEORGE CROOM ROBERTSON, 23 letters, 1867–1892.
Robertson papers, U.C.L.

HENRY SIDGWICK, three letters, 1891–1897.
Sidgwick papers, Trinity College, Cambridge.

BEATRICE WEBB (and members of the Potter family), 39 letters, 1853–1903.
Passfield papers, L.S.E.

Printed Material

DAVID DUNCAN, *Life and Letters of Herbert Spencer* (London, 1908).

HERBERT SPENCER, *Works*, 19 vols. (London, 1861–1902).

HERBERT SPENCER, *An Autobiography*, 2 vols. (London, 1904).

DNB 1901–1911, 360; *ESS* XIV 295; *IESS* XV 121.

Portraits: B.M.(P); N.P.G.; L.S.E.; S.N.P.G.

THOMAS SPRING-RICE, 1st BARON MONTEAGLE, 1790–1866

Personal papers, including much correspondence on politics, poor laws, colonies, finance, etc., 1820–1866. Also notes for speeches, letter books, and registers of letters received.
N.L.I., MSS. 532–543, 555–562, 545–553, 11140, 13345–13413.

A group of letters to Spring-Rice on political topics, 1825–1856.
N.L.S., MS. 2225.

Family correspondence, including some letters to and from his son Charles, 1835–1866.
Manchester J.R.U.L., MS. 1187.

Correspondents

MATTHEW AYLMER, 5th Baron Aylmer, five items (copies), 1834.
B.M. Add. MSS. 43236–43237.

CHARLES BABBAGE, 12 items, 1835–1847.
B.M. Add. MSS. 37189–37201.

HENRY PETER BROUGHAM, 1st Baron Brougham and Vaux, 56 letters, 1825–1864.
Brougham papers, U.C.L.

GEORGE CANNING, several letters, 1823–1824.
Canning papers, Leeds City Library, Archives Dept.

BENJAMIN DISRAELI, Earl of Beaconsfield, seven letters, 1852.
Disraeli papers, N.R.A. 0842.

HENRY RICHARD VASSALL FOX, 3rd Baron Holland, several letters, 1833–1844.
B.M. Add. MS. 51573.

WILLIAM EWART GLADSTONE, *c.* 100 items, 1852–1865.
B.M. Add. MSS. 44372–44406.

GEORGE HAMILTON GORDON, 4th Earl of Aberdeen, seven items, 1834–1853.
B.M. Add. MSS. 43236–43251.

CHARLES GREY, 2nd Earl Grey, 18 letters, 1831–1835.
Grey of Howick papers, Durham D.P.

HENRY GEORGE GREY, 3rd Earl Grey, 32 letters, 1831?–1845.
Grey of Howick papers, Durham D.P.

WILLIAM HUSKISSON, five items, 1827–1828.
B.M. Add. MSS. 38996–39114.

EDWARD JOHN LITTLETON, 1st Baron Hatherton, four letters, 1833–1834.
Hatherton collection, Staffordshire R.O.

SAMUEL JONES LOYD, Baron Overstone, three letters, 1844–1858.
Overstone papers, London U.L., MS. 804.

MACVEY NAPIER, 69 letters, 1830–1846.
B.M. Add. MSS. 34614–34626.

SIR JOHN NEWPORT, 14 letters, 1827–1842.
Newport MSS., Queen's University, Belfast.

ROBERT OWEN, five letters, 1837–1858.
Owen correspondence, Co-operative Union Ltd, Manchester.

SIR ROBERT PEEL, *c.* 85 items, 1818–1849.
B.M. Add. MSS. 40275–40602.

HENRY CRABB ROBINSON, six items, 1838–1856.
Crabb Robinson papers, Dr Williams' Library, London.

LORD DUDLEY COUTTS STUART, four letters, 1838–1839.
Harrowby papers, N.R.A. 1561.

HENRY JOHN TEMPLE, 3rd Viscount Palmerston, eight letters, 1837–1846.
Broadlands papers, N.R.A. 12889.

SIR ROBERT JOHN WILMOT-HORTON, 24 letters, 1826–1834.
Catton collection, Derby Borough Library.

CHARLES WOOD, 1st Viscount Halifax, 14 letters, 1835–1851.
Hickleton papers, N.R.A. 8128.

THOMAS WYSE, two letters, n.d.
N.L.I., MS. 15025.

Printed Material
DNB XVIII 835; Boase II 931.

Portraits: B.M. (P); N.P.G. (A).

SIR JAMES STEUART-DENHAM, BT, 1712–1780

Two manuscript memoirs of Steuart, the manuscripts of works, notes on money, credit and coinage, extracts from commonplace books and a small group of letters.

Coltness papers. (Microfilm at Edinburgh U.L.)

A criticism of Hume's *Tudor History*, *c* 1760. Not in Steuart's hand.
N.L.S., MS. 9376.

Corrected and revised copies of the *Inquiry* and other works.
L.S.E.

Another copy of the manuscript of the *Inquiry*.
Badische Landsbibliothek, Karlsruhe.

Correspondents

DAVID ERSKINE, 11th Earl of Buchan, two letters, 1780.
Edinburgh U.L.

DAVID ERSKINE, 11th Earl of Buchan, two letters, 1780–1783.
N.L.S., MS. 2956.

SIR PHILIP FRANCIS, two letters, 1776–1777.
India Office Library, Home Misc. 62.

DAVID HUME, one letter, 1767.
Hume MSS., Royal Society of Edinburgh.

WILLIAM PITT the Younger, four letters, n.d.
Chatham papers, P.R.O.

JAMES FRANCIS EDWARD STUART, Chevalier de St George, 28 items, 1740–1756.
Stuart papers, Windsor.

SAMUEL WILKS, 15 letters, 1772.
India Office Library, Home Misc. 62.

Printed Material

PAUL CHAMLEY, *Documents Relatifs à Sir James Steuart* (Strasbourg, 1965).

SAMAR R. SEN, *The Economics of Sir James Steuart* (London, 1957).

SIR JAMES STEUART, *An Inquiry into the Principles of Political Economy*, ed. Andrew S. Skinner (Edinburgh, 1966).

Palgrave III 475; *DNB* V 793; *ESS* XIV 389; *IESS* XV 265.

Portrait: see *Inquiry* (above).

DUGALD STEWART, 1753–1828

Some letters to and from Stewart, travel journals, 1797–1803; one or two other manuscripts and sets of notes from his lectures on moral philosophy or political economy, 1793–1794, 1797, 1801–1802, 1806–1807, 1808–1809.
Edinburgh U.L.

Notes from his lectures on political economy, 1803–1804.
N.L.S., MS. 3771.

Notes from his lectures on political economy, 1806.
London U.L., MS. 150.

Two volumes of notes from his lectures on moral philosophy, 1785–1786.
Aberdeen U.L.

Notes from his lectures on political economy, 1802–1803 (in the handwriting of Lord Palmerston).
Library of the London Museum.

Notes from his lectures on political economy, 1802–1803.
Seligman collection, Columbia U.L., New York.

Correspondents

HENRY PETER BROUGHAM, 1st Baron Brougham and Vaux, two letters, 1811.
Brougham papers, U.C.L.

ARCHIBALD CONSTABLE, several letters, 1809–1820.
N.L.S., MS. 675.

BARON DE GERANDO, 1792–1816.
N.L.S., MS. 5319.

F. W. GILMER, two letters, 1824.
Gilmer family papers, University of Virginia Library, Charlottesville.

JOHN HALKETT, three letters, 1817.
N.L.S., MS. 546.

LADY JANE HOME, a few letters, 1777–1786.
Home MSS., N.R.A. 10169.

SIR JAMES MACKINTOSH, two letters, 1812 and n.d.
B.M. Add. MSS. 52451–52452.

JOHN MANDERSTON, six items, 1820.
B.M. Add. MS. 34612.

MACVEY NAPIER, ten letters, 1811–1820.
B.M. Add. MSS. 34611–34612.

ADAM SMITH, one letter, n.d.
Glasgow U.L.

JOHN STARK, nine letters, 1810–1820.
Edinburgh U.L.

Printed Material

The Collected Works of Dugald Stewart, ed. Sir William Hamilton, 11 vols. (Edinburgh, 1854–1860).

MATTHEW STEWART, *Memoir of the Late Dugald Stewart* (Edinburgh, 1838).

Palgrave III 476; *DNB* XVIII 1169.

Portraits: see *Collected Works* and M. Stewart (above).

RICHARD HENRY TAWNEY, 1880–1962

24 boxes of lectures in typescript and manuscript, for history and economic history courses and for various special occasions, 1910–1950. Some notes for books and pamphlets, and a few items of correspondence.
Tawney papers, L.S.E.

60 boxes of economic history notes and transcripts from documents.
Dept. of Economic History, L.S.E.

Correspondents

WILLIAM HENRY BEVERIDGE, Baron Beveridge, many letters, 1903–1961.
Beveridge papers, L.S.E.

EDWARD C. CARTER, four letters, 1938.
Columbia U.L., New York.

SIR RICHARD DOUGLAS DENMAN, 46 letters, 1900–1929.
Beveridge papers, India Office Library.

JOHN LAWRENCE LE BRETON HAMMOND, 16 letters, 1917–1947.
Bodleian, MS. Hammond.

ARTHUR CREECH JONES, 90 letters, 1929–1961.
Creech Jones papers, Rhodes House Library, Oxford.

JOHN MAYNARD KEYNES, Baron Keynes, 14 letters, 1912–1946.
Keynes papers, Marshall Library, Cambridge.

BRIAN PEARCE, 11 letters, 1938–1941.
L.S.E.

SIR WILLIAM ROTHENSTEIN, four letters, 1934–1942.
Houghton Library, Harvard University.

EDWIN ROBERT ANDERSON SELIGMAN, two letters, 1920–1929.
Seligman papers, Columbia U.L., New York.

GRAHAM WALLAS, six letters, 1914–1924.
Wallas papers, L.S.E.

SIDNEY and BEATRICE WEBB, nine letters, 1933–1947.
Passfield papers, L.S.E.

Printed Material

R. H. Tawney's Commonplace Book, ed. J. M. Winter and D. M. Joslin (London, 1972).

IESS xv 518.

THOMAS PERRONET THOMPSON, 1783–1869

Papers mainly connected with his periods in Sierra Leone and the Persian Gulf, but including some on his political and economic interests. Collections by two descendants for projected biographies contain more of his papers, and copies of material from other sources.
Thompson papers, Hull U.L.

11 letters to various correspondents, 1824–1864.
Edinburgh U.L.

Letters to and from Thompson, 1808–1868, some with family, but also ten to George Pryme, 1811–1866, and one to Joseph Hume, 1838. Some miscellaneous notes by Thompson, and correspondence, etc., of other members of the family, some of which relates to him.
T. P. Thompson collection, Brotherton Library, Leeds University.

Correspondents

ANTI-CORN LAW LEAGUE, five letters, 1838–1839.
League letter books, Manchester City Library.

JEREMY BENTHAM, three letters, 1830.
B.M. Add. MS. 33546.

THOMAS CHALMERS, four letters, 1832.
Chalmers papers, New College, Edinburgh.

RICHARD COBDEN, *c.* 100 letters, 1841–1861.
B.M. Add. MS. 43663.

GEORGE JACOB HOLYOAKE, four letters, 1854–1865.
Holyoake collection, Co-operative Union Ltd, Manchester.

AUGUSTUS DE MORGAN, five items, 1846–1862.
London U.L., A.L. 337.

H. B. PEACOCK, 208 letters (including some to Peacock's daughters), 1844–1855.
Manchester J.R.U.L., MS. 1180.

FRANCIS PLACE, *c.* 20 items, 1829–1845.
B.M. Add. MSS. 35145–35151.

JOHN BENJAMIN SMITH, three letters, 1836–1837.
J. B. Smith papers, Manchester City Library.

WILLIAM WHEWELL, five letters, 1829–1840.
Whewell papers, Trinity College, Cambridge.

SIR ROBERT JOHN WILMOT-HORTON, four letters, 1830–1831.
Catton collection, Derby Borough Library.

GEORGE WILSON, 17 letters, 1843–1847.
Wilson papers, Manchester City Library.

Printed Material

LEONARD G. JOHNSON, *General T. Perronet Thompson* (London, 1957).

Palgrave III 535; *DNB* XIX 704; Boase III 942.

Portraits: B.M. (P); N.P.G. (A); see Johnson (above).

CHARLES EDWARD POULETT THOMSON, BARON SYDENHAM, 1799–1841

Thomson's papers passed to his brother Poulett Scrope, who willed them to his nephew Hugh Hammersley, with his own. These papers are not now held by the Hammersley family, nor do they seem to have been deposited with any institution.

Some letters and papers on the formation of a School of Design, 1836–1839.
B.M. Add. MS. 31218.

Four volumes of correspondence, 1831–1834, on commercial negotiations with France, from John Bowring and George William Frederick Villiers (later 4th Earl of Clarendon) to Thomson.
Bodleian, MS. Clar. Dep. c546.

The Board of Trade papers contain many letters to and from Thomson on official business.
P.R.O.

Despatches to Sydenham as Governor-General of Canada from the Colonial Office, despatches from Lieutenant-Governors to him, letter books of his despatches to the Colonial Office, letter books of internal correspondence, and much other miscellaneous relating to his period as Governor-General.
Governor-General of Canada Office papers, Canadian Public Archives.

Some commissions and patents, with three letters to Sydenham and one from him, 1836–1841.
Sydenham papers, Canadian Public Archives.

Correspondents

WILLIAM EDEN, 1st Baron Auckland, two letters, 1834.
B.M. Add. MS. 34460.

EDWARD ELLICE, 17 letters, n.d.
Ellice papers, N.L.S.

CHARLES GREY, 2nd Earl Grey, three letters, 1832.
Grey of Howick papers, Durham D.P.

HENRY GEORGE GREY, 3rd Earl Grey, 18 letters, 1834–1840.
Grey of Howick papers, Durham D.P.

SIR JOHN HARVEY, three letters, 1839–1840.
Harvey papers, Canadian Public Archives.

JOHN CAM HOBHOUSE, 1st Baron Broughton, four letters, 1835–1837.
B.M. Add. MSS. 36467–36468.

SIR JAMES PHILLIPS KAY-SHUTTLEWORTH, four letters, 1833–1834.
Kay-Shuttleworth papers, Manchester J.R.U.L.

JOHN GEORGE LAMBTON, 1st Earl of Durham, eight letters, 1832–1839.
Durham papers, Canadian Public Archives.

SIMON MCGILLVRAY, five letters, 1839.
Canadian Public Archives, MG19 A-35.

ROBERT OWEN, three items, 1839.
Owen correspondence, Co-operative Union Ltd, Manchester.

LORD JOHN RUSSELL, 1st Earl Russell, 47 letters, 1839–1841.
Russell papers, P.R.O.

JOHN BENJAMIN SMITH, three letters, 1834–1837.
J. B. Smith papers, Manchester City Library.

HENRY JOHN TEMPLE, 3rd Viscount Palmerston, 15 letters, 1831–1840.
Broadlands papers, N.R.A. 12889.

GEORGE WILLIAM FREDERICK VILLIERS, 4th Earl of Clarendon, six letters, 1831–1833.
Bodleian, MS. Clar. Dep. c545.

RICHARD COLLEY WELLESLEY, 1st Marquess Wellesley, two letters, 1836–1837.
B.M. Add. MS. 37311–37312.

Printed Material

GEORGE POULETT SCROPE, *Memoir of the Life of Charles, Lord Sydenham* (London, 1843).

ADAM SHORTT, *Lord Sydenham* (London, 1926).

DNB XIX 716.

Portraits: B.M. (P); see Shortt (above).

HENRY THORNTON, 1760–1815

The Thornton family papers include letters, 1777–1815, and diaries, 1795–1814, of Henry Thornton, mostly copies.
Cambridge U.L., Add. MS. 7674.

Another set of copies of his letters and diaries, by his daughter Marianne.
Wigan R.O.

A copy of *Paper Credit*, with notes interleaved, probably for a new edition.
Baker Library, Harvard University.

Correspondents

JEREMY BENTHAM, four letters, 1798.
B.M. Add. MS. 33542.

THOMAS CLARKSON, *c.* 150 letters, 1791–1793.
B.M. Add. MSS. 41262A, 41263.

WILLIAM PITT the Younger, six letters, n.d.
Chatham papers, P.R.O.

THOMAS PERRONET THOMPSON, several letters, 1804–1813.
Thompson papers, Hull U.L.

JOHN VENN, seven letters, 1791–1796.
Venn MSS., Church Missionary Society, London.

Printed Material

STANDISH MEACHAM, *Henry Thornton of Clapham* (London, 1964).

Palgrave III 537; *DNB* XIX 781; *IESS* XVI 14.

Portrait: N.P.G. (A).

THOMAS TOOKE, 1774–1858

Enquiries made to direct descendants of Tooke (since deceased) by the editors of Ricardo's *Works* established that no papers were held by the family, nor have any been found in institutions.

Five letters to Tooke from different correspondents, 1833.
Chadwick papers, U.C.L.

Correspondents

CHARLES BABBAGE, five letters, 1832–1844.
B.M. Add. MSS. 37186–37193.

ALEXANDER BLAIR, copies of two items, 1842.
B.M. Add. MS. 40540.

JOHN ELLIOT CAIRNES, two letters, 1857.
N.L.S., MS. 8944.

WILLIAM HUSKISSON, three items, 1825–1827.
B.M. Add. MSS. 38747–38752.

SAMUEL JONES LOYD, Baron Overstone, two letters, 1857.
Overstone papers, London U.L., MS. 804.

R. PAGE, two letters, 1839.
Bodleian, MS. Eng. Lett. b3.

HENRY BROOKE PARNELL, 1st Baron Congleton, a few letters, *c.* 1840.
Congleton papers.[12]

DAVID RICARDO, three letters, 1821.
Ricardo papers, Cambridge U.L., Add. MS. 7510.

THOMAS SPRING-RICE, 1st Baron Monteagle, two letters, 1854.
N.L.I., MS. 13401.

SIR ROBERT JOHN WILMOT-HORTON, 28 letters, 1825–1831.
Catton collection, Derby Borough Library.

MARMADUKE WYVILL, two letters, 1844.
Wyvill papers, North Riding R.O.

Printed Material
Palgrave III 548; *DNB* XIX 974; Boase III 987; *ESS* XIV 651; *IESS* XVI 103.

Portrait: N.P.G. (A).

ROBERT TORRENS, 1780–1864

Extensive efforts by scholars over the years have failed to trace Torrens's papers. Direct descendants have been contacted without success.

Correspondents
WILLIAM HENRY ARCHER, three letters, 1847–1864.
Archer papers, National Library of Australia, MS. 71.

HENRY PETER BROUGHAM, 1st Baron Brougham and Vaux, 14 letters, 1831–1860.
Brougham papers, U.C.L.

BENJAMIN DISRAELI, Earl of Beaconsfield, 11 letters, 1847–1850.
Disraeli papers, N.R.A. 0842.

SIR JAMES GRAHAM, copies of several letters, n.d.
Graham papers, N.R.A. 2634.

JOHN GEORGE LAMBTON, 1st Earl of Durham, five letters, 1831–1839.
Lambton papers, Alexander Turnbull Library, Wellington, New Zealand.

SAMUEL JONES LOYD, Baron Overstone, 60 letters, 1847–1863.
Overstone papers, London U.L., MS. 804.

SIR ROBERT PEEL, nine items, 1841–1845.
B.M. Add. MSS. 40486–40557.

SIR JOHN GEORGE SHAW-LEFEVRE, four letters, 1837 and n.d.
Shaw-Lefevre papers, House of Lords R.O.

EDWARD GIBBON WAKEFIELD, three items, 1839.
Lambton papers, Alexander Turnbull Library, Wellington, New Zealand.

SIR ROBERT JOHN WILMOT-HORTON, 20 letters, 1826–1831.
Catton collection, Derby Borough Library.

CHARLES WOOD, 1st Viscount Halifax, ten letters, 1848–1860.
Hickleton papers, N.R.A. 8128.

Printed Material

LIONEL C. ROBBINS, *Robert Torrens and the Evolution of Classical Economics* (London, 1958).

Palgrave III 550; *DNB* XIX 993; Boase III 991; *ESS* XIV 652; *IESS* XVI 105.

EDWARD WAKEFIELD, 1774–1854

Letters concerning the marriages of Wakefield himself, and of his son Edward Gibbon Wakefield, 1816–1824. Some letters and other papers on mental hospitals, 1814–1816.
Wakefield papers.[1]

Correspondents

HENRY PETER BROUGHAM, 1st Baron Brougham and Vaux, five letters, 1823–1836.
Brougham papers, U.C.L.

GEORGE EDEN, two letters, 1813.
B.M. Add. MS. 34458.

JOHN FOSTER, 1st Baron Oriel, 28 letters, 1805–1807.
Foster/Massereene papers, P.R.O.N.I.

WILLIAM HONE, three letters, 1813–1814.
B.M. Add. MS. 40120.

SIR ROBERT PEEL, six letters, 1844–1845.
B.M. Add. MSS. 40550–40570.

FRANCIS PLACE, *c.* 15 letters, 1813–1817.
B.M. Add. MSS. 35152–35153.

DAVID RICARDO, many letters, 1815–1823.
Ricardo papers, Cambridge U.L., Add. MS. 7510.

ARTHUR YOUNG, 21 letters, 1802–1816.
B.M. Add. MSS. 35123–35133.

Printed Material
Palgrave III 647; *DNB* xx 448; Boase III 1129.

EDWARD GIBBON WAKEFIELD, 1796–1862

Travel journals for Italy, 1816–1818, and France and Italy, 1836; letters to members of the family, manuscript articles and other papers, 1816–1841. Many letters to Catherine Torlesse, 1824–1852.
Wakefield and Torlesse papers.[1]

12 letters between Wakefield and various correspondents, 1830–1850. Copies of Wakefield family correspondence from collections in other libraries, 1837–1854. Minute book and letter book of the New Zealand Association, 1837–1838, the latter containing out-letters by Wakefield.
Mitchell Library, Sydney, New South Wales.

Various letters of Wakefield, to different correspondents.
Canterbury Museum, Christchurch, New Zealand.

Copies of a few items of family correspondence relevant to Wakefield.
B.M. Add. MS. 35261.

Annotated copies of settlements, bonds and related correspondence, 1817–1827, resulting from his marriage.
Lockwood Estate papers, Essex R.O.

Papers relating to his attempt to trace Thomas Berkely Bond in Paris, 1825–1828.
Archives Nationales, Paris. (Microfilm in Archives Dept., Public Library of South Australia, Adelaide.)

Seven letters to various correspondents, 1823–1851.
City of Wellington Public Library, New Zealand.

Correspondents

HENRY SAMUEL CHAPMAN, two letters, 1842.
Alexander Turnbull Library, Wellington, New Zealand, MS. papers 53.

JAMES EDWARD FITZGERALD, 59 letters 1849–1852.
Alexander Turnbull Library, Wellington, New Zealand, MS. papers 64.

LOUIS HIPPOLYTE LA FONTAINE, three letters, 1838–1843.
La Fontaine papers, Municipal Library, Montreal.

WILLIAM EWART GLADSTONE, four items, 1836–1851.
B.M. Add. MSS. 44355–44370.

HENRY GEORGE GREY, 3rd Earl Grey, three items, 1831–1837.
Grey of Howick papers, Durham D.P.

ROWLAND HILL, two letters, 1834.
B.M. Add. MS. 38109.

JAMES HENRY LEIGH HUNT, two letters, 1834.
B.M. Add. MSS. 38109, 38523.

JOHN GEORGE LAMBTON, 1st Earl of Durham, eight letters, 1838–1839.
Durham papers, Canadian Public Archives.

JOHN GEORGE LAMBTON, 1st Earl of Durham, ten letters, 1837–1839.
Lambton papers, Alexander Turnbull Library, Wellington, New Zealand.

GEORGE WILLIAM LYTTELTON, 4th Baron Lyttelton, 36 letters, 1850–1854.
Alexander Turnbull Library, Wellington, New Zealand, MS. papers 222.

DENIS BENJAMIN VIGER, two letters, 1842.
Viger papers, Canadian Public Archives.

GEORGE FREDERICK YOUNG, three letters, 1849.
Royal Commonwealth Society, London, MS. 89.

Printed Material

The Collected Works of Edward Gibbon Wakefield, ed. M. F. Lloyd-Prichard (Glasgow, 1968).

PAUL BLOOMFIELD, *Edward Gibbon Wakefield: Builder of the British Commonwealth* (London, 1961).

Palgrave III 648; *DNB* xx 449; Boase III 1129; *ESS* xv 322.

Portraits: B.M.(P); N.P.G.; Canterbury Museum, New Zealand.

SIDNEY JAMES WEBB, BARON PASSFIELD, 1859–1947

Papers of Sidney and Beatrice Webb from before and during their married life. Much political correspondence, drafts of speeches, articles for publication, etc. There is material connected with their many interests, such as L.S.E., the Fabian Society and the *New Statesman*.
Passfield papers, L.S.E.

Correspondence and despatches on Malta, between Webb, Sir Harry Charles Luke and Sir John Du Cane, 1930–1931.
Luke papers, Rhodes House Library, Oxford.

Some papers connected with various aspects of the Labour Party.
Papers of the Labour Party, N.R.A. 14863.

Correspondents

ALBERT VICTOR ALEXANDER, 1st Earl Alexander, several letters, 1924–1939.
Alexander papers, Churchill College, Cambridge.

HERBERT HENRY ASQUITH, Earl of Oxford and Asquith, six letters, 1895–1909.
Bodleian, MS. Asquith.

WILLIAM HENRY BEVERIDGE, Baron Beveridge, many letters, 1905–1944.
Beveridge papers, L.S.E.

JAMES BRYCE, Viscount Bryce, several letters, 1891–1918.
Bryce papers, Bodleian.

JOHN BURNS, 24 letters, 1889–1908.
B.M. Add. MS. 46287.

EDWIN CANNAN, five letters, 1889–1931.
Cannan collection, L.S.E.

RICHARD THEODORE ELY, several letters, 1880s and 1890s.
Ely papers, University of Wisconsin, Madison.

SIR ROBERT ENSOR, two letters, 1903–1912.
Ensor papers, Corpus Christi College, Oxford.

FABIAN SOCIETY, many letters, 1891–1939.
Fabian Society papers, Nuffield College, Oxford.

HUBERT HALL, ten letters, 1902–1932.
L.S.E.

JOHN LAWRENCE LE BRETON HAMMOND, six letters, 1923–1944.
Bodleian, MS. Hammond.

WILLIAM ALBERT SAMUEL HEWINS, 18 letters, 1895–1903.
Hewins papers, Sheffield U.L.

JOHN KELLS INGRAM, two letters, 1892–1906.
Ingram papers, P.R.O.N.I.

JOHN MAYNARD KEYNES, Baron Keynes, four items, 1920–1922.
Keynes papers, Marshall Library, Cambridge.

JOHN MAYNARD KEYNES, Baron Keynes, five letters, n.d.
Keynes papers, King's College, Cambridge.

CHARLES ARTHUR PARKER, four letters, 1912–1913.
Bodleian, MS. Eng. Lett. d269.

SIR HORACE PLUNKETT, nine letters, 1910–1928.
Plunkett papers, Plunkett Foundation, Oxford.

Political Science Quarterly, 14 letters, 1888–1902.
Political Science Quarterly papers, Columbia U.L., New York.

PAUL R. REYNOLDS, *c.* 150 letters, 1913–1946.
Reynolds papers, Columbia U.L., New York.

HERBERT LOUIS SAMUEL, 1st Viscount Samuel, 11 letters, 1892–1943.
Samuel papers, House of Lords R.O.

EDWIN ROBERT ANDERSON SELIGMAN, 29 letters, 1890–1929.
Seligman papers, Columbia U.L., New York.

GEORGE BERNARD SHAW, ten letters, 1883–1938.
B.M. Add. MS. 50553.

EDWARD DARWIN SIMON, Baron Simon, several letters, 1909–1940.
Simon papers, Manchester City Library.

GRAHAM WALLAS, *c.* 150 letters, 1891–1928.
Wallas papers, L.S.E.

Printed Material

BEATRICE WEBB, *My Apprenticeship* (London, 1926).

BEATRICE WEBB, *Our Partnership*, ed. Margaret I. Cole and Barbara Drake (London, 1941).

BEATRICE WEBB, *Beatrice Webb's Diaries, 1912–1924*, ed. Margaret I. Cole (London, 1952).

BEATRICE WEBB, *Beatrice Webb's Diaries, 1924–1932*, ed. Margaret I. Cole (London, 1952).

DNB 1941–1950, 935; *IESS* XVI 487.

A biography of Sidney and Beatrice Webb by Royden Harrison is forthcoming; and a definitive edition of the Webbs' correspondence is in prospect.

Portraits: N.P.G.; L.S.E.; see Beatrice Webb (above).

RICHARD WHATELY, 1787–1863

A volume of letters received and drafts, copies and originals of letters sent (including seven to Nassau Senior, 1818–1841), 1818–1861. Also notes, memoranda and poems.
Whately papers, Lambeth Palace Library, London, MS. 2164.

Copies of three dialogues on reasoning.
N.L.W., Harpton Court papers, 3554.

Four letters to various correspondents, 1854–1857.
Houghton Library, Harvard University.

Correspondents

JOHN GEORGE BERESFORD, *c.* 30 items, 1833–1859.
Beresford papers, Trinity College, Dublin.

HENRY PETER BROUGHAM, 1st Baron Brougham and Vaux, five items, 1831–1836.
Brougham papers, U.C.L.

ARTHUR HUGH CLOUGH, three letters, n.d.
Bodleian, MS. Eng. Lett. c189, c190, d175.

EDWARD COPLESTONE, three letters, 1821–1825.
Hawkins papers, Oriel College, Oxford.

EDWARD GRANVILLE ELIOT, 3rd Earl of St Germans, copies of six items, 1853.
B.M. Add. MS. 43207.

CAROLINE FOX, several letters, 1836–1842.
B.M. Add. MS. 51965.

GEORGE HAMILTON GORDON, 4th Earl of Aberdeen, *c.* 20 items, 1853.
B.M. Add. MSS. 43250–43251.

CHARLES GREY, 2nd Earl Grey, 30 letters, 1832–1834.
Grey of Howick papers, Durham D.P.

SIR WILLIAM ROWAN HAMILTON, 26 items, 1837–1863.
Hamilton papers, Trinity College, Dublin.

EDWARD HAWKINS, 54 letters, 1823–1861.
Hawkins papers, Oriel College, Oxford.

CHARLES THOMAS LONGLEY, two letters, 1847–1863.
Longley papers, Lambeth Palace Library, London.

MACVEY NAPIER, six letters, 1828–1842.
B.M. Add. MSS. 34613–34623.

JOHN HENRY NEWMAN, seven items, 1834.
Newman papers, Oratory of St Philip Neri, Birmingham.

SIR ROBERT PEEL, six items, 1829–1842.
B.M. Add. MSS. 40399–40499.

ADAM SEDGWICK, five letters, 1860.
B.M. Egerton MS. 3020.

NASSAU WILLIAM SENIOR, many letters, 1811–1859.
Nassau Senior papers, N.L.W.

SAMUEL WILBERFORCE, five letters, 1846–1861.
Bodleian, MSS. Wilberforce.

SIR ROBERT JOHN WILMOT-HORTON, two letters, 1829–1830.
Catton collection, Derby Borough Library.

Printed Material

WILLIAM JOHN FITZPATRICK, *Memoirs of Richard Whately*, 2 vols. (London, 1864).

ELIZABETH JANE WHATELY, *The Life and Correspondence of Richard Whately*, 2 vols. (London, 1866).

Miscellaneous Remains from the Commonplace Book of Richard Whately, ed. Elizabeth Jane Whately (London, 1864).

Palgrave III 663; *DNB* xx 1334; Boase III 1295; *ESS* xv 407.

Portraits: B.M.(P); N.P.G.(A); see *Centenary History of the Statistical and Social Inquiry Society of Ireland*, ed. R. D. Collison Black (Dublin, 1947).

WILLIAM WHEWELL, 1794–1866

Notes, lectures and manuscripts of published and unpublished works on mathematical, scientific, philosophic, economic and other topics. Correspondence of several thousand items on the above topics as well as college, university and personal matters. Some of his own letters (including 285 to Richard Jones, 1817–1854) have been returned and added to these papers.
Whewell papers, Trinity College, Cambridge.

Letters, reports on papers, and manuscripts of papers.
Royal Society Library, London.

Letters and accounts on university business.
Cambridge University Archives.

17 letters between Whewell and different correspondents, 1838–1856.
Houghton Library, Harvard University.

Correspondents

CHARLES BABBAGE, ten letters, 1820–1847.
B.M. Add. MSS. 37182–37201.

HENRY PETER BROUGHAM, 1st Baron Brougham and Vaux, three items, 1834–1849.
Brougham papers, U.C.L.

WILLIAM BUCKLAND (and Mrs Buckland), eight letters, 1831–1848.
Buckland papers, Royal Society Library, London.

EDWARD GEORGE EARLE LYTTON BULWER-LYTTON, Baron Lytton, four letters, 1865–1866.
Bulwer-Lytton papers, Hertfordshire R.O.

JAMES DAVID FORBES, *c.* 140 letters, 1831–1865.
Forbes correspondence, St Andrews U.L.

EDWARD HAWKINS, 30 letters, 1842–1865.
Hawkins papers, Oriel College, Oxford.

SIR JOHN FREDERICK WILLIAM HERSCHEL, 65 letters, 1817–1866.
Herschel papers, Royal Society Library, London.

JOHN GIBSON MCVICAR, five letters, 1852–1864.
Library of the Royal College of Physicians, London.

AUGUSTUS DE MORGAN, three letters, 1849–1861.
De Morgan papers, London U.L., MSS. 775, 776.

SIR ROBERT PEEL, six items, 1841–1845.
B.M. Add. MSS. 40492–40576.

ADOLPHE QUÉTELET, 34 letters, 1832–1861.
Quetélet papers, Bibliothèque Royale de Belgique, Brussels.

HENRY CRABB ROBINSON, two letters, 1840–1847.
Crabb Robinson papers, Dr Williams' Library, London.

WILLIAM SOMERVILLE, seven letters, 1831–1833 (and six to Mary Somerville, 1832–1839).
Somerville papers, Bodleian.

THOMAS SPRING-RICE, 1st Baron Monteagle, 26 items, 1850–1854.
N.L.I., MS. 13401.

SAMUEL WILBERFORCE, seven letters, 1845–1869.
Bodleian, MSS. Wilberforce.

Printed Material

JANET M. DOUGLAS, *The Life and Selections from the Correspondence of William Whewell* (London, 1882).

ISAAC TODHUNTER, *William Whewell: An Account of his Writings with Selections from his Literary and Scientific Correspondence* (London, 1876).

Palgrave III 665; *DNB* xx 1365; Boase III 1301; *IESS* xvi 531.

Portraits: B.M. (P); N.P.G.; Trinity College, Cambridge.

PHILIP HENRY WICKSTEED, 1844–1927

Wicksteed by his own admission kept 'next to no documents'.

A few manuscript and typescript fragments, two letters to, and one letter from Wicksteed, with some printed pamphlets.
Wicksteed papers, L.S.E.

Correspondents

BASIL BARNHILL, two letters, 1925.
Houghton Library, Harvard University.

EDWIN CANNAN, six letters, 1922–1927.
Cannan collection, L.S.E.

JAMES MACLUCKIE CONNELL, 18 letters, 1911–1926.
Dr Williams' Library, London.

HERBERT STANLEY JEVONS, four letters, 1907.
Jevons papers, Manchester J.R.U.L.

SIR D'ARCY WENTWORTH THOMPSON, six letters, 1904–1925.
Thompson papers, St Andrews U.L.

GRAHAM WALLAS, 15 letters, 1894–1922.
Wallas papers, L.S.E.

LÉON WALRAS, six letters, 1884–1889.
Fonds Walras, Bibliothèque Cantonale et Universitaire, Lausanne.

KNUT WICKSELL, four letters, 1906–1922.
Wicksell papers, Lund Universitetsbibliotek, Sweden.

Printed Material

CHARLES H. HERFORD, *Philip Henry Wicksteed* (London, 1931).

ESS xv 418; *IESS* xvi 544.

Portrait: see Herford (above).

SIR ROBERT JOHN WILMOT-HORTON, BT, 1784–1841

Correspondence, in chronological sequence for the most part, with copies of some out-letters. The correspondence of economic interest falls mainly in the period 1823–1831.
Catton collection, Derby Borough Library.

The records of the Colonial Office contain many papers connected with Wilmot-Horton's work.
P.R.O.

Correspondents

GEORGE CANNING, several letters, 1822–1827.
Canning papers, Leeds City Library, Archives Dept.

GEORGE HAMILTON GORDON, 4th Earl of Aberdeen, three items, 1829–1830.
B.M. Add. MSS. 43233–43234.

HENRY GEORGE GREY, 3rd Earl Grey, four letters, 1831.
Grey of Howick papers, Durham D.P.

WILLIAM HUSKISSON, *c.* 30 items, 1823–1828.
B.M. Add. MSS. 38745–38754.

AUGUSTA LEIGH, a few letters, 1824.
B.M. Add. MS. 31037.

GRANVILLE LEVESON-GOWER, 1st Earl of Granville, 80 letters, 1817–1838.
Granville papers, P.R.O.

SIR HUDSON LOWE, *c.* 100 items, 1822–1826.
B.M. Add. MSS. 56088–56091.

SIR ROBERT PEEL, *c.* 300 items, 1822–1830.
B.M. Add. MSS. 40346–40401.

GEORGE RAMSAY, 9th Earl of Dalhousie, copies of letters, 1824–1825.
Dalhousie papers, Scottish R.O.

HENRY JOHN TEMPLE, 3rd Viscount Palmerston, two letters, 1827–1829.
Broadlands papers, N.R.A. 12889.

Printed Material

R. N. GHOSH, 'The Colonisation Controversy: R. J. Wilmot-Horton and the Classical Economists', *Economica*, N.S., XXXI (1964) 385.

DNB IX 1284.

Portrait: B.M.(P).

JAMES WILSON, 1805–1860

Wilson's papers seem to have been destroyed by a descendant, and the destruction of the archives of the *Economist* by fire during the Second World War removed the other important source of information about him.

Correspondents

EDWARD GEORGE EARLE LYTTON BULWER-LYTTON, Baron Lytton, ten letters, 1844–1856.
Bulwer-Lytton papers, Hertfordshire R.O.

RICHARD COBDEN, five letters, 1839–1846.
B.M. Add. MS. 43667.

WILLIAM EWART GLADSTONE, *c.* 150 items, 1853–1855.
B.M. Add. MS. 44346.

GEORGE HAMILTON GORDON, 4th Earl of Aberdeen, about ten items, 1853–1854.
B.M. Add. MSS. 43251, 43254.

HENRY GEORGE GREY, 3rd Earl Grey, 33 letters, 1847–1856.
Grey of Howick papers, Durham D.P.

HENRY JOHN TEMPLE, 3rd Viscount Palmerston, four letters, 1850–1857.
Broadlands papers, N.R.A. 12889.

GEORGE WILLIAM FREDERICK VILLIERS, 4th Earl of Clarendon, 14 letters, 1853–1856 (and 11 letters from Clarendon to Wilson, 1847–1854, MS. Eng. Lett. e91).
Bodleian, MS. Clar. Dep. c1–c82.

GEORGE WILSON, seven letters, 1840–1846.
Wilson papers, Manchester City Library.

CHARLES WOOD, 1st Viscount Halifax, three volumes of correspondence, 1859–1860.
Halifax papers, India Office Library.

Printed Material
EMILIE BARRINGTON, *The Servant of All* (London, 1927).

Palgrave III 669; *DNB* XXI 571; Boase III 1413.

Portraits: N.P.G.; see Barrington (above).

ARTHUR YOUNG, 1741–1820

Eight volumes of correspondence, 1743–1820, mainly letters to Young, but also *c.* 100 out-letters. The manuscripts for his unpublished treatise, the 'Elements and Practice of Agriculture'.
B.M. Add. MSS. 34821–34864, 35126–35133.

A few items of family correspondence, including 15 letters from his son, the Rev. Arthur Young, mainly to Young himself. Also 11 leaves of his autobiography which did not appear in the published version.
Bagshawe Muniments, Manchester J.R.U.L.

13 letters, 1770–1802, and volumes of minutes which reflect Young's work for the Royal Society of Arts.
Royal Society of Arts Library, London.

The manuscripts of the Board of Agriculture include letters of Young, and minute books from his period with the Board.
Royal Agricultural Society of England, Kenilworth.

Correspondents

SIR JOSEPH BANKS, six letters, 1789–1791.
Royal Botanic Gardens Library, Kew.

SIR JOSEPH BANKS, 26 letters, 1786–1799.
Yale U.L.

SIR JOSEPH BANKS, eight letters, 1789–1804.
California State Library, Sutro Branch.

JEREMY BENTHAM, eight letters, 1794–1797.
B.M. Add. MSS. 33541, 33542.

SIR JAMES CALDWELL, six letters, 1772–1779.
Bagshawe Muniments, Manchester J.R.U.L.

MARIANNE FRANCIS, *c.* 100 letters, 1811–1820.
Burney papers, Berg collection, New York Public Library.

GEORGE O'BRIEN, 3rd Earl of Egremont, 26 letters, 1793–1815.
Petworth House Archives, N.R.A. 15719.

WILLIAM PITT the Younger, five letters, 1796–1799.
Chatham papers, P.R.O.

THOMAS RUGGLES, 12 letters, 1795–1811.
Ruggles-Brise papers, N.R.A. 1019.

GEORGE WASHINGTON, six letters, 1786–1794.
Washington papers, Library of Congress.

PHILIP YORKE, 3rd Earl of Hardwicke, ten letters, 1799–1819.
B.M. Add. MSS. 35643–35700.

Printed Material

The Autobiography of Arthur Young with Selections from his Correspondence, ed. M. Betham-Edwards (London, 1898).

Palgrave III 687; *DNB* XXI 1272; *ESS* XV 515.

Portraits: B.M.(P); N.P.G.

INDEX OF NAMES

Page numbers in Italics indicate a main entry.